# BITCOIN
## IS FOR
# EVERYONE

# BITCOIN
# IS FOR
# EVERYONE

### Why Our Financial System is
### Broken and Bitcoin is the Solution

# Natalie Brunell

# Harriman House

HARRIMAN HOUSE LTD
Website: harriman.house

First published in 2025 by Harriman House, an imprint of Pan Macmillan
Associated companies throughout the world
www.panmacmillan.com

Copyright © Natalie Brunell 2025

The right of Natalie Brunell to be identified as the author has been asserted in accordance with the Copyright, Design and Patents Act 1988.

Paperback ISBN: 978-1-80409-113-5
eBook ISBN: 978-1-80409-114-2

Figure 1, 2, 3, 5, 6, 8, 9 and 10 were created by the author using ChatGPT generative AI tools. Figures 4 and 7 were drawn by the publisher, but feature graphics created by the author using ChatGPT generative AI tools.

Cover design by Charlotte Smith and images by AdobeStock.

01

Printed in the United States of America.

Everyone is against Bitcoin
before they are for Bitcoin.

—MICHAEL SAYLOR

# CONTENTS

# PREFACE

"There are these two young fish swimming
along and they happen to meet an older fish
swimming the other way, who nods at them
and says 'Morning, boys. How's the water?'
And the two young fish swim on for a bit, and
then eventually one of them looks over at the
other and goes, '*What the hell is water?*'"

DAVID FOSTER WALLACE

---

## Everyone could use a roadmap.

WE'RE SWIMMING IN a world as inseparable from money as fish from water.

We work, spend, save, and strive, but rarely pause to ask the question that could change everything:

"*What the heck is money?*"

→⟩⟩

The moment we start questioning money—not just how to get more of it, but what it really *is*—we begin to see the world differently. This book is an invitation to take that first look.

As its title suggests, *Bitcoin is for Everyone* is for, well, everyone. From those living paycheck-to-paycheck to families with comfortable savings and even investors overseeing multi-million-dollar portfolios, we all grapple with the challenges brought on by today's economic system.

Many of us feel like we're steering a ship that's taking on water, just one strong wave away from sinking altogether. For others, keeping afloat still requires constant effort: investing wisely, taking on debt, and relying on complex strategies just to stay ahead.

We've come to accept all of this as "normal," but it's worth asking: does it really have to be this way?

This book explores how we got to this point and offers a simple, relatable introduction to Bitcoin as a way out of our losing battle with *broken money*, a concept we'll define and unpack throughout the book.

It offers a path to righting that ship.

⇝

Bitcoin is getting a lot of attention these days, and its role in the global economy will only become more significant in the decades to come. Learning about Bitcoin is eye-opening and inspiring, but it can also feel daunting: with so much information out there, it's easy to feel confused, overwhelmed, or unsure of where to begin.

That's why I wrote this book.

You don't need a background in economics or technology—or to be an investigative journalist like me—to understand Bitcoin's potential. You just need a bit of curiosity and an open mind.

⇝

We'll begin our Bitcoin journey with a portrait of our current financial system, uncovering the flaws that have led to such extreme wealth concentration and a pervasive sense of frustration among those left behind.

Once we're oriented in the world of broken money, we'll be prepared to recognize Bitcoin not just as an alternative to the status quo, but as a groundbreaking, transformational instrument of financial empowerment. We'll peek under the hood and explore the nuts and bolts of Bitcoin—what it is, where it came from, and how it works—while keeping our eye on the larger problems it was explicitly designed to solve.

Lastly, we'll examine how Bitcoin opens up the potential for freedom and flourishing in places where financial oppression has long precluded such possibilities, and consider how Bitcoin helps reframe the way we create and experience value in our own lives. Of course, we'll also discuss methods of buying and storing the bitcoin token itself.

⟶»

*Bitcoin is for Everyone* invites you to challenge that status quo and reflect on how we've been conditioned to accept the way things *are* rather than imagine the way they *could be*.

By the time you finish this book, I hope you'll see what I see: that Bitcoin is a barrier-breaking tool for financial freedom, helping regular people like you and me to navigate away from those turbulent financial waters and build real, lasting wealth.

My goal is to teach you about Bitcoin so you can begin to reimagine your own dreams—because building a better future starts with believing it's possible.

The journey begins here.

# INTRODUCTION: EVERYONE HAS A STORY

> "Life sometimes brings enormous difficulties
> and challenges that seem just too hard to
> bear. But bear them you can, and bear them
> you will, and your life can have a purpose."
>
> BARBARA WALTERS

T HINK ABOUT HOW many times your day has already crossed paths with money. Did you stop for coffee or gas? Buy groceries for dinner? What about the clothes you're wearing, the water bottle you filled, or even the chair you sat on at work?

Money is woven into nearly every aspect of our lives. Tucking in the kids, curling up with a good book, or scrolling on your phone before turning out the lights? The blanket, pillow, pajamas, wall paint, book, smartphone, Wi-Fi, stuffed animal, and, of course, those lights: money earned, money spent, sometimes even the feeling of money wasted.

Money flows through everything, stitching together the fabric of our daily existence so seamlessly that we hardly notice—that is, until it no longer stretches far enough.

⇛

With our jobs, school conferences, oil changes, and dental appointments, we rarely have the time to stop and consider the nature of money itself.

We know what money is.

*Don't we?*

⇛

Most of us have a pretty complicated relationship with money. And if we don't like to *think* about it, then we really don't like to *talk* about it, especially when times are tough.

Financial struggles can leave us feeling inadequate, ashamed, and vulnerable.

We may assume that, deep down, we only have ourselves to blame for our problems. We work hard to make sure nobody knows about our financial stress, and respond with our most convincing "I'm good!" when anyone asks.

The anxious, sinking feeling in our gut tells an entirely different story. While we struggle, everyone else seems to be making it work—*aren't they?*

While this book is about Bitcoin and how to build lasting financial security, at its core, it's really a book about *hope*.

In many ways, money and hope are two forces that propel our lives forward; like all of us, my own life has been shaped by both.

⇛

Since she was very young, my mother's dream was to come to America. My parents grew up in Communist Poland, where people suffered through the hostilities of war, an oppressive government, and multiple invasions. There was little sense of economic opportunity or social mobility.

To this day, my mom vividly recalls standing in endless food lines with young children in tow. On one occasion, after finally reaching the counter following hours of waiting, she was devastated to learn that the woman ahead of us had taken the last parówki—my favorite little hot dogs. I burst into tears, my mom did too, and the kind stranger was moved to offer us some of her parówki. That was life under Communism.

My late grandfather introduced my mom to classic American films, radio programs, and other glimpses of life beyond the Iron Curtain—planting a seed in her mind that a better world might exist. He told her that in America, there was freedom and opportunity; a place where people didn't have to wait hours in line for basic necessities, and where children could dream of achieving more than their parents ever could.

Back in Poland, my family lived under complete centralized control, in a world of constant shortages. People had to get creative to make ends meet, often turning to the underground economy because there were no other options.

It might sound cliché, but for them, just knowing that America was out there felt like a beacon in the night.

⟶

I was only five years old when we arrived in Chicago from Poland, but some memories are etched in my mind.

I remember our first apartment outside the city—it wasn't much. Just two tiny bedrooms, one bathroom, and a cramped kitchen where my mom somehow managed to produce elaborate Polish dishes no matter how busy she was with work. My parents insisted that my brother and I take the bedrooms, wanting us to feel a sense of normalcy and privacy, while they made do with a cheap sofa bed in the living room.

I didn't fully appreciate the weight of that selflessness and sacrifice until I was much older.

—⟫—

Back then, I thought being "rich" simply meant having a garage. My dad, an electrician, worked six days a week and would wake up at 3 a.m. during Chicago's brutal winters to scrape the ice and snow off the car. Seeing him brave the freezing cold—day after day and year after year—fueled the conviction they'd long instilled in me: that hard work and education were the path to a better life. I was determined to honor all they'd sacrificed by seizing every opportunity that came my way.

As I grew up, my parents encouraged me to pursue a career in medicine, law, or even government—fields they associated with stability and financial security. But I had other ideas. The TV news was always on in our home, not just to keep us informed, but to help my parents learn English. Watching those broadcasts, I felt drawn to the idea of telling stories that mattered. I decided I wanted to become a journalist like Barbara Walters or Oprah Winfrey, to meet people from all walks of life and share their stories with the world.

Little did I know that the financial earthquake that would become the global story of the decade was also about to upend my own personal and professional life.

—⟫—

By the time I entered high school, my parents—encouraged by the norms of their adopted American culture—had gradually shifted from saving in *cash*, an ingrained habit from decades spent under Communist rule, to using *credit*—borrowing from banks to pursue their dreams.

This was a major adjustment, as they had grown up in a system where such borrowing was almost unheard of: in Communist Poland, there were no credit cards or mortgages, and housing was typically allocated by the government. If you somehow managed to buy a home, it was paid for upfront in cash. The very idea of using borrowed money to build a life was completely foreign to my parents.

So when they eventually purchased their modest townhome in the suburbs of Chicago, my parents' mortgage not only symbolized their embrace of the American dream, but also their newfound trust in this unfamiliar system.

⟶⟩

That was a golden age for our family. My mom and dad finally had their own bedroom and even, incredibly, a garage! Over the next few years, their trust in the American way only deepened. Home values were skyrocketing—increasing nearly 35% between 2004 and 2006 alone[1]—and it ultimately seemed foolish not to follow their friends' example and leverage the low interest rates and increased home values to their advantage. So my parents finally set aside their doubts and took out a home equity loan to start the little Polish eatery and deli market my mom had dreamed of opening since immigrating.

They had barely finished stocking the shelves when, like a tsunami, the Great Financial Crisis of 2008 washed away everything.

⟶⟩

We lost our home. My parents filed for bankruptcy. They've never fully recovered, financially or emotionally. The financial crisis broke their nest egg, their hopes, and ultimately their relationship.

To this day, it's hard for me to write or talk about this experience without a wave of deep sadness. It marked a clear pivot point in my life: almost overnight, my wide-eyed confidence in a bright, promising future was lost to the stark realities of adulthood in a world that made no sense.

Witnessing the collapse of my parents' lives in real time changed everything for me. I felt betrayed: how could this happen to good, honest people? To my family—and untold millions like us—who had worked so hard and played by the rules?

⇢⇢

My family's experience of sudden financial devastation lit a fire in me. Naturally, I looked for someone to blame. My anger turned immediately toward the "rich and the greedy." I assumed they had used their power and influence to manipulate the government into bailing them out with hundreds of billions of taxpayer dollars— money quietly siphoned from meager paychecks like ours.

I empathized with the Occupy Wall Street movement, which called for taxing the wealthy and redistributing the money to those of us in need. I have always felt for the "little guy," crushed under the weight of a system rigged in favor of the powerful, and resolved to do something about it. I would, indeed, become an investigative journalist just like my heroines, shining a light on the injustices and corruption that so many endured in silence.

Over the next ten years, I poured myself into that mission, criss-crossing the country to interview those "little guys" for my stories—ordinary people like my parents, trying to navigate a system stacked against them. I exposed public corruption, the soaring costs of living and education, and the growing polarization that was already beginning to tear communities apart.

↠

I loved my job. The work was fascinating, but also heartbreaking; the people I interviewed deserved so much more. We all did.

My reporting earned accolades and awards, but even after a decade of "paying my dues," I still barely made enough to cover my bills, much less save for my future. The pit in my stomach never went away.

With every story and with each passing year, I was haunted by the same feeling: something just wasn't right. The future—once so thrilling to contemplate—felt utterly discouraging.

It was the opposite of everything I had believed about the American Dream, which had promised a better life through hard work and perseverance.

I couldn't possibly have known it at the time, but those difficult years were preparing me to recognize the discovery that would change my life. Though, like so many of our greatest insights, it would take some time to fully appreciate that.

↠

I first encountered Bitcoin through friends in 2016, and even covered it briefly on local TV[2] in Sacramento, California the following year. Around the same time, I bought a little—not out of conviction, but as a gamble.

**Back then I was stuck in the paradigm of the broken system, treating Bitcoin as little more than a lottery ticket. I didn't yet realize that it might be the best solution to the very problems I was trying to escape and expose.**

It wasn't until a few years later, as I was trying to get a handle on my financial situation, that I finally picked up the Bitcoin books my mentor had been urging me to read.

As I read, the pieces started falling into place. I felt like a veil was lifted from over my eyes. So many things started to click.

I began to understand the true nature of the issues I'd been reporting on throughout my career: the people I interviewed weren't failing because they didn't work hard enough or because of bad luck. Like me, they were actually trapped in financial quicksand.

I began to realize that Bitcoin wasn't a gamble at all; it was a lifeline.

→»

Learning about Bitcoin changed my life. It opened my eyes to the root causes behind the problems I had been questioning: *why* is the American Dream slipping away? *Why* is everything getting more expensive? *Why* have so many people lost hope? It made me realize that many of our basic assumptions about money—what it is and how it works—are flawed.

Our leaders may tell us the economy is strong, but the facts on the ground, in our homes and in our wallets, tell a different story.

Whether we blame ourselves, our political enemies, or some vague notion of misfortune, we know in our bones that something is wrong, and we feel helpless.

→»

For years, I had reported on major events—economic crises, political shifts, social unrest—without fully understanding the one force silently shaping them all: *money*. I didn't yet have the tools to recognize how the monetary system drives so much of what we see in the headlines. Bitcoin gave me that lens—and once I saw it,

I couldn't look away. That's why I left a promising career in legacy television journalism to educate people about Bitcoin.

It not only revealed the cause of so many of our problems, but also provided a solution: a new foundation for economic empowerment available to all of us.

I knew I couldn't keep this discovery to myself. Bitcoin gave me hope when I'd felt hopeless, and I knew that sharing this knowledge with the world was no longer merely aligned with my long-standing mission to help ordinary people. It was my *calling*.

# 1.
# EVERYONE
# SENSES THERE'S
# A PROBLEM

**"A nickel ain't worth a dime anymore."**

YOGI BERRA

———————

**E**ACH YEAR, THE same amount of money buys us less and less. That coffee on the way to work, the groceries on the way home, healthcare, car repairs, the cost of buying a house—nearly everything we need keeps getting more expensive.

This pattern feels so ingrained in our reality that we've come to see it as inevitable. After all, our parents paid much less for milk, homes, and college tuition than we do today—and our grandparents paid even less than that.

If you're like me, you've probably shrugged this off as beyond your control, chalking up rising costs to "just the way things are."

But have you ever stopped to wonder *why*? Why is everything getting more expensive while our ability to keep up feels like it's slipping away?

→»

Even if we receive an annual raise, many of us still struggle to keep pace with living expenses—let alone make meaningful strides toward financial security or building wealth.

This relentless financial squeeze is especially heartbreaking because it runs counter to the very promise that so many of us, no matter where in the world we happen to live, grew up believing in: the American Dream. This ideal occupies a unique and sacred place in history, offering the hope of *a life defined by our efforts, not our circumstances.*

But achieving that dream today is another story. Like a child with a coloring book, many of us try our best to stay "inside the lines" of what we can afford. But the boundaries keep closing in, and the dream eludes us.

Something *is* dreadfully wrong.

→»

Wealth concentration in the United States has surpassed that of almost every other major developed nation.[3]

Wages have barely risen over the last few decades.[4] What's worse, adjusted for inflation, they're actually hovering at just about the same rate they were 40 years ago!

One-in-eight among us are living in poverty.[5]

Meanwhile, in just the four years between March 2020 and December 2024, the combined wealth of America's top billionaires *increased* by more than 193%![6]

**These aren't just numbers. They paint a stark picture of a system that continues to widen the gap between the haves and the have-nots.**

⇢⇢

You don't need to be an economist to recognize that the top 1% of Americans have amassed more wealth than the entire middle class, the undisputed backbone of society.

If this angers you, you're not alone.

This wealth concentration isn't because the "have-nots" have suddenly become lazy and incompetent. Or because the "haves" suddenly got extra greedy. There has always been greed and there always will be.

The problem lies in how money itself has been corrupted.

As billionaire Wall Street mogul Carl Icahn put it in an HBO documentary, "I made this money because the system is so bad, not because I'm a genius."[7]

He nailed it.

The fact that winners keep increasing their share of the pie while the rest of us fight over (fewer and fewer) crumbs is actually a symptom of the problem beneath all of the others: broken money.

Icahn's observation also points to a deeper truth. Even for those who feel that money is working just fine—where spending is as easy as swiping a credit card and investments grow steadily—a society that's structurally impoverished by a broken financial system is inherently fragile.

And the cracks in our social foundation are becoming pretty hard to ignore.

⇢⇢

It wasn't supposed to be this way. This isn't the world we thought we were inheriting from our parents and grandparents.

Most of us were raised to believe that even when times were tough, a strong work ethic promised the chance at a better life for ourselves, our families, and our communities. But the goalposts keep moving.

For those holding down multiple jobs who *still* find that they're forced to take on debt to keep up with basic necessities, it just doesn't add up.

And among those enjoying the comforts of financial success, the consequences are still very real: how long can society hold together under the weight of a growing majority pushed to the brink by frustration and despair?

⇢

To me, the American Dream embodies the hope my parents felt when they imagined coming to the United States. My mom would say that, back home in Poland, if you were born poor, you likely died poor. But in America, you could come from poverty—or arrive here with absolutely nothing—and with a strong work ethic and education, you could achieve absolutely anything. Years later, I'd come to meet other children of immigrant families who grew up hearing the exact same thing—and believing it, too.

This was the life my mother longed for, the life she moved heaven and earth to create for her family.

The fact that there is a country dedicated to those ideals, however imperfectly—one literally founded on the premise that the pursuit of freedom and happiness is the highest expression of human potential—has widened the lens on what is possible. It has attracted untold millions to America, unleashed vast reservoirs of human energy and ingenuity, and *it has changed the world.*

It's the one dream big enough to hold all others, and it's a dream worth fighting for. The American Dream is named for the country that has come to symbolize it most, but the dream really is *universal.*

→»

That dream, however, is deeply in trouble.

When the cost of living rises so dramatically[8] that credit card debt hits all-time highs and delinquencies climb—especially among young adults—it's clear that something has gone very wrong.

When over half of Americans are saddled with medical debt (even those with insurance![9]), we know that something has gone very wrong.

When the skyrocketing cost of food brings tens of millions of Americans to food pantries[10] for support, we know that something has gone very wrong.

But perhaps nowhere is the faltering American Dream more evident than in the prospect of homeownership. Once a cornerstone of stability, homeownership is now out of reach for nearly half of all Americans due to soaring real estate prices,[11] forcing a quarter of millennials—my generation—to move back in with their parents.[12]

This hopelessness shows: a recent, startling survey from the University of Michigan found that young Americans are 50% more likely to question whether life has a purpose. Four in ten stated it's "hard to have hope for the world."[13]

Social media brims with emotional videos of young people who don't know how they'll ever be able to afford a home, or even be able to raise children without financial strain.

→»

These are not the cries of the spoiled or greedy. They are heartfelt expressions of frustration and despair from a generation who can point to the modest, comfortable homes of their middle-class upbringing—now almost completely unattainable, with conservative estimates suggesting that over just the five years between 2020 and 2025, *incomes would have had to rise 79% in order to buy a typical home*[14]—as clear evidence of an economy gone awry.

And this burden doesn't stop with them. Younger generations face the crushing weight of skyrocketing college costs, while their parents delay retirement, working far beyond the years once reserved for rest. Even those with stable, well-paying jobs often find themselves juggling second or third incomes just to keep up with mounting rents and ever-increasing expenses.

As you can see in Figure 1, in 1971 a single middle-class income was enough to afford a nice home. The situation today looks very different.

**Figure 1: Median income and median home price in 1971 and 2025**

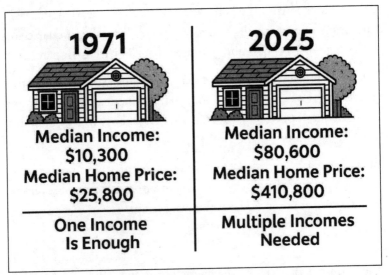

Source: United States Census Bureau, "Money Income in 1971" (December 1972); Federal Reserve Bank of St. Louis (2025).

Though we try to put on a brave face, our hearts are heavy with worry.

⇝

When you break down issues to the level of basic human experience, we all have so much in common. We crave connection and a sense of belonging. We want to improve our lives today while saving for a brighter tomorrow; we want a quality education for our children, safer communities, a place we're proud to call home; we want the time we put into our jobs to be valued and compensated fairly. We also want to make sure that our families and the people who depend on us will be cared for when we're gone.

These are not idle fantasies; they are the foundation of a healthy society. So it's worth asking why many of us feel that the promise of this land of opportunity is vanishing, and why the ripple effects of this loss are felt far beyond America's shores.

⇝

While global conversations have shifted into binary "us versus them" political battles, the fingerprints of our broken monetary system are everywhere.

The gap between the rich and everyone else isn't just growing; it's widening at an accelerating rate, making it impossible to catch up. If we're chasing a car that's gaining speed, at some point, it becomes impossible to close the gap.

It's why our yearly raises—if we're lucky enough to get them—fall so short. As we'll see in Chapter Two, those raises simply aren't keeping up with our loss of purchasing power.

None of this is natural or unavoidable.

⇝

But we're getting ahead of ourselves. As the saying goes, "A problem defined is a problem half solved."* When we've only known one system for our entire lives, it can be difficult to clearly perceive it.

As a reporter, I was on a mission to uncover and expose the wrongs I saw all around me.

But, like the two young fish oblivious to water, I was so focused on the symptoms of broken money that I never thought to examine the system itself.

I didn't realize that money, the very foundation of our economy, was controlled by a select few who could expand its supply and alter its value with a mere keystroke. I didn't realize how deeply the ever-growing supply of money has affected every aspect of my life. The system was stacking the odds against people like me, while making it easier than ever for those at the top to continue growing their wealth.

But recognizing how this system affects the cost of living, the value of time, and the scope of our dreams is the first step toward reimagining it.

⇸

_____

* This quote has been cited in various forms by a number of people. Most frequently it is attributed to Charles Kettering, Vice President and Director of Research for General Motors from 1920 to 1947.

# Chapter 1 Summary

Our money buys less and less each year. We blame ourselves for falling behind. The cost of living has skyrocketed, and basic necessities, like housing, now demand multiple incomes when one used to feel like it was enough. This is not because we're lazy or irresponsible, but because we're living within a system of *broken money*—a system where most people work hard but barely get ahead, where wages don't keep up with rising prices, and where quality of life declines from one generation to the next. Understanding the nature of this problem is the first step toward reclaiming economic opportunity and reviving the American Dream.

**Key Takeaway**: The rising cost of living isn't your fault—it's the result of a broken monetary system that leads to extreme wealth concentration.

# 2.
# EVERYONE'S WORKING HARDER FOR LESS

*"It isn't what we don't know that gives us trouble, it's what we know for sure that just ain't so—like thinking a dollar will always be worth a dollar."*

JOSH BILLINGS

---

**M**OST OF US grew up hearing that we should work hard and save money. The idea was simple: if you put away part of your paycheck, over time you'll secure your future.

Benjamin Franklin famously said, "A penny saved is a penny earned." But today, it's more accurate to say that a penny saved is a penny lost. Simply earning a paycheck and saving in cash isn't enough anymore, and I wish I'd learned that sooner.

With the slow erosion of purchasing power that defines today's economy, money tucked away in a piggy bank or basic checking account loses value day by day, like an ice cube melting in the sun. For many, even saving into a workplace retirement plan isn't enough to ensure financial stability.[15]

This means that if you want to stay afloat (let alone get ahead), you can't just *save* money; **you have to *invest* it in things that grow in value**.

You'll have to acquire *assets* like stocks, real estate, gold, or even small businesses—anything that can appreciate or generate income faster than prices rise.

In other words, *you need your money to work for you*, just to keep up with the rising cost of living.

→»

But how many of us have actually learned this? For those who didn't attend business school, the nuts and bolts of investing—both the *why* and the *how*—often remain overwhelming and mysterious.

So most wage earners (people who trade their time for a paycheck) have followed the age-old advice to work hard and save what they can, yet still find themselves falling behind.

To even preserve their standard of living, everyday workers must find a way, without any training or guidance, to become part-time investors.

As Michael Saylor, Executive Chairman of Strategy observed, "A person should not be required to speculate on central bank policy, boardroom politics, competitive dynamics, technology trends, regulatory interference, congressional politics, labor relations, litigation, and nation state conflicts just to preserve their life savings."[16]

That melting ice is pushing us into a race most of us never signed up for.

⇉

In recent years, I've watched friends take on debt to buy investment properties, aiming to improve their financial standing. Real estate has traditionally been a powerful wealth-building tool, and with good reason, but it's far from simple. Managing properties—whether for long-term rentals or short-term stays—requires time, expertise, and constant effort, all while navigating risks, maintenance costs, and other financial complexities.

Most of these friends never aspired to have a side hustle as a landlord. But as *Forbes* succinctly put it, "The global citizen has to work twice as hard thinking about money and how it can be tweaked to preserve and/or grow value."[17]

⇉

Whether we're aware of it or not, broken money has pushed us into a never-ending chase for *yield*—the preferred term, among professionals, for *"return on investment."*

We rarely stop to question what is actually happening, and why.

**The answer comes down to *inflation*, but not the kind that makes the headlines. This inflation takes place long before we see prices rise.**

⇉

We've spent our entire lives under the spell of inflation, accepting it as a given: prices go up! After all, that's what's been happening since our grandparents paid a quarter for bread and $1.50 for a movie (see Table 1).

**Table 1: 1971 cost of living**

| Living | |
|---|---|
| New house | $25,200 |
| Average income | $10,622 per year |
| New car | $3,560 |
| Average rent | $150 per month |
| Tuition to Harvard University | $2,600 per year |
| Movie ticket | $1.50 each |
| Gasoline | 40¢ per gallon |
| United States postage stamp | 8¢ each |

| Food | |
|---|---|
| Granulated sugar | 62¢ for 5 pounds |
| Vitamin D milk | $1.17 per gallon |
| Ground coffee | 98¢ per pound |
| Bacon | 80¢ per pound |
| Eggs | 45¢ per dozen |
| Fresh ground hamburger | 62¢ per pound |
| Fresh baked bread | 25¢ per loaf |

Source: www.wtfhappenedin1971.com.

While inflation is often discussed in terms of rising prices, that's only part of the story. At its core, inflation is a loss of purchasing power. And it's driven not by natural forces, but by an expanding money supply.

→»

More to the point: while rising prices represent the *effect* of inflation, they're not actually the *cause*.

The deeper source of our problems—the story we don't hear much about—is that ever-expanding supply of money. This is called *monetary inflation*, also known as *currency debasement*. For reasons we'll soon explore, when more money is created, each dollar becomes less valuable over time. The result? Prices go up, meaning your money doesn't stretch as far as it used to.

**Monetary inflation is the hidden engine behind the soaring cost of many of life's essentials.**

Now you might be thinking, "Wait, there are plenty of reasons prices go up! What about supply chain disruptions or tariffs?" While these factors can certainly cause prices to rise, they're often the well-publicized, near-term shocks—not the root cause.

The truth is, beneath those surface-level forces lies a deeper, more persistent current. The steady and relentless increase in the overall money supply is quietly eroding the value of our dollars.

↦

Take a look around: prices on everything we need—groceries, homes, insurance—have been climbing far faster than our paychecks.

Many groceries have nearly doubled over the last few years; a home that cost $60,000 in 1970—brand new!—now costs $500,000, while probably needing a complete remodel. What was once affordable on one middle-class income now requires two, or even three.

We feel the sting everywhere, but most of us aren't in a position to explore the systemic causes of our problems. We shrug our shoulders, vent to friends and family, or complain on social media. We assume someone "out there" is incredibly greedy—maybe a corporation, maybe the "super-rich"—and we go back to doing the best we can to make it all work.

After all, inflation is just a fact of life, right?

→»

Rising prices wouldn't be so damaging if incomes rose at the same pace. But as we'll see, **when the money supply expands, the new money created in the system doesn't reach everyone equally**. It flows in a very specific direction, benefiting some people (the wealthy and well-connected) while hurting others (the rest of us).

Workers rarely see any of that new money in the form of meaningful wage increases. Instead, it accumulates in fewer and fewer hands, driving up the price of assets owned by the wealthy, while putting enormous financial pressure on the vast majority of us over time.

And yet, even as technology continues to create efficiencies that *should* make everything cheaper for us, inflation remains the bedrock of our entire debt-based economic system.

→»

Governments and central banks promote a "healthy" 2% annual inflation rate as necessary to keep the economy stable and growing.

The idea, they say, is that mild inflation encourages spending and investment and gives policymakers room to stimulate the economy when needed. This target isn't just embraced in the United States— it's the norm in most countries around the world.

That 2% refers to *consumer price inflation* (CPI, which actually stands for *Consumer Price Index*, the metric used to measure and document that inflation). CPI tracks the cost of things like food, clothing, cars, and other daily essentials. Anything higher than that 2% figure tends to stoke public frustration, but anything lower signals a slowing economy.

You've probably seen the constant news reports: inflation is rising, cooling, stabilizing, spiking. It's enough to make your head spin! But even when reports indicate that "inflation is coming down," it doesn't mean prices are falling. **It just means they're rising more slowly**.

People might assume that policymakers are earnestly trying to eliminate or reduce inflation. The reality is that inflation in this system isn't a temporary glitch to be resolved; it's actually baked in by design.

This puts us all on a moving walkway that speeds up 2% every year.

↦

Here's the data: averaging the CPI's year-over-year changes from 2000 onward, inflation works out to about 2.5% per year—very close to the official target.

This average even accounts for the post-pandemic spike, when CPI hit 9.1% in June 2022.[18]

**Yet most of us know that our own bills and expenses have climbed far higher than 2.5%, especially in recent years**.

If you've given CPI any thought at all, you probably assume, as I once did, that it reflects an accurate portrait of all types of inflation, including the ballooning cost of housing—but it doesn't.

For instance, college tuition increased by an average of 5.5% per year since 2000,[19] annual premiums for employer-sponsored family health coverage by an average of 6% per year,[20] and healthcare spending by 5.5% per year during that time.[21]

You may have also noticed that home prices have surged beyond that target inflation rate; since 2000, the median home price in the U.S. has increased by more than 4% annually, and in some regions by an average of more than 7% per year.[22]

Meanwhile, wages have roughly paralleled the stated CPI, showing only 3% annual growth since 2000.[23]

**So while your paycheck might tick upward a bit each year, it definitely isn't keeping up with the rising costs of education, healthcare, and housing.**

And the gap between what you earn and what life costs just keeps widening.

**Table 2: Long-term price growth, 2000-2025**

| Category | Compound Annual Growth Rate (CAGR) 2000–2025 |
|---|---|
| Headline CPI | 2.5 % |
| Median wages | 3.0 % |
| Median home price | 4.1 % |
| College tuition & fees | 5.5 % |
| Healthcare spending | 5.5 % |
| Health coverage premiums | 6.0% |

Source: "2024 Employer health Benefits Survey," KFF, (October 2024), www.kff.org.

⤕⤕

So why is there a disconnect between the official inflation rate and the rising prices we actually experience?

The fact is, the CPI tracks the prices of a hypothetical "basket of goods" representing everyday purchases, *but the contents of that basket are often cherry-picked and continually rearranged.*

When steak gets too expensive, statisticians assume that shoppers will just buy chicken instead. So they just replace "steak" with "chicken" in their calculations and claim the cost of living stayed the same. When a new car offers better safety tech or a bigger screen, the CPI treats it as "getting more for your money," a bit of financial wizardry that makes it look like the price actually went down.

Other adjustments also contribute to the mismatch. Sizes quietly shrink ("shrinkflation"), and rent—the largest expense in most household budgets—is, jaw-droppingly, calculated by asking a sampling of homeowners to essentially "guesstimate" how much they'd rent their homes for if they decided to do so. Together, these silent tweaks help to preserve the "safe" 2% target, even as our real-world expenses climb much faster.

The point is: the inflation numbers being reported to us don't match the reality we're experiencing.

⇶

Even if inflation really were just 2% a year—and we know it's not—that seemingly small number would still quietly erode our purchasing power over time. And this doesn't even take into account the power of *compounding*. In reality, the true cost increases are far higher.

Like a boat taking on water at a slow and steady rate, 2% inflation would probably feel manageable at first. But as the water starts to accumulate faster than you can remove it, each new inch adds to the load you're already struggling to manage. Over time, you're not just bailing out what leaked in this year—you're dealing with water that's been building up for years. That's how compounding inflation works: it quietly increases your burden, until you're barely staying afloat.

What starts as a small inconvenience builds into a crisis as purchasing power is drained from our savings, salaries, and pensions. Over time, the result is clear: even when we're doing everything "right," we're still sinking.

Because of compounding, the consequences of even minor monetary inflation become quickly magnified. It means that after 35 years, the purchasing power of our money gets cut in half.

## Chart 1: How compounding affects purchasing power at 2%

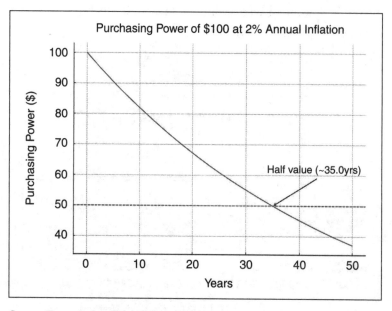

Source: Example from Natalie Brunell to illustrate compound interest calculation.

Let's pause right there. You may be wondering: "If there's more money to go around each year, isn't that good for everyone? Doesn't it make everyone richer?"

It's a fair question. While it might be a bit counterintuitive, adding more money to the system doesn't translate to more wealth for everyone. Instead, for most of us, adding money to the system actually dilutes its value.

Picture a glass of fine red wine. If you add just a splash of water—say, 2%—you might not notice much of a difference at first. But keep adding water, year after year, and eventually, the wine becomes unrecognizable. The color fades, the flavor disappears, and you're left with a weak, watered-down version of the original. You'll eventually need a bigger glass to hold it all!

But here's the catch. You don't actually have more wine—you have increasingly diluted wine, which is on its way to becoming little more than flavored water.

**Figure 2: Inflation acts like dilution**

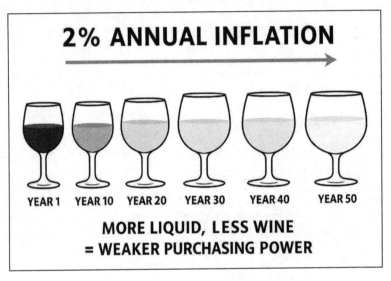

That's exactly what happens with monetary inflation. As we will soon explore, the nature of money is such that as its supply expands, the purchasing power of each unit (in this case, the dollar) is incrementally diluted.

↦

Say you own a rare trading card—one of only 21 ever printed. Its value comes from that built-in scarcity; collectors know they'll have to bid against each other to score one. Now, picture a factory suddenly churning out hundreds of identical copies. Overnight, what was once quite rare is now practically commonplace. Because the supply has exploded, the market price of your original card collapses.

Money works in much the same way. When the supply of dollars grows faster than the supply of goods and services available for purchase, each individual dollar commands a smaller slice of real value, and its "collectibility" drops. Just as flooding the market with more cards dilutes their worth, flooding the economy with new dollars dilutes each dollar's purchasing power. You need more of them to pay for the same groceries, rent, or concert tickets.

↦

And it gets even worse. As we touched on earlier, *new money isn't distributed evenly throughout the economy*. Instead, it's piped in the direction of those closest to its source: powerful institutions, large corporations, and the financial elite.

We'll see how this creates an uneven playing field, filling the glasses of those at the top with rich red wine while everyone else is left with dull, watered-down runoff.

↦

# Chapter 2 Summary

We grew up thinking that hard work and saving money would secure our future. But today, that formula no longer works. Quietly and steadily, inflation erodes the value of every dollar we earn. Official numbers like the CPI might suggest that things are stable, but those figures are adjusted in ways that mask the true rise in living costs. Meanwhile, wages have failed to keep up, and ordinary people are forced into the role of reluctant investors— buying real estate, stocks, or anything else that might outpace inflation—just to preserve their purchasing power.

**Key Takeaway**: You're not falling behind because you made bad choices. You're falling behind because the system is designed to shrink the value of your money over time.

# 3.
# EVERYONE SHOULD'VE LEARNED THIS IN SCHOOL

"The best investment you can make is in yourself.
The more you learn, the more you'll earn."

WARREN BUFFETT

I N THE LAST chapter, we saw how the official CPI number often hides the real bite of inflation. Now let's zoom out even further and look at the source of that pain: a system that floods the economy with new money and concentrates wealth at the top.

Economists use a measure called "M2" to count our total money supply. Think of M2 as every dollar that could be spent in the near future—cash in our wallets and checking accounts ("M1")—plus most savings accounts and retail money-market funds. All told, M2 shows how much ready-to-use money is available in the economy.

→»

The chart below illustrates how dramatically the U.S. M2 money supply has expanded since 1971—an important year we'll revisit in Chapter Eight. When we plot the growth of the money supply over time, one takeaway jumps off the page: M2 has marched in a relentless one-way climb, steadily diluting the purchasing power of every dollar already in circulation along the way.

And if we focus on just the last five years, you'll notice a massive shift in 2020, when the Covid rescue packages kicked in and the money supply shot almost straight up.

**Chart 2: Rate of M2 money supply growth 1971–2025**

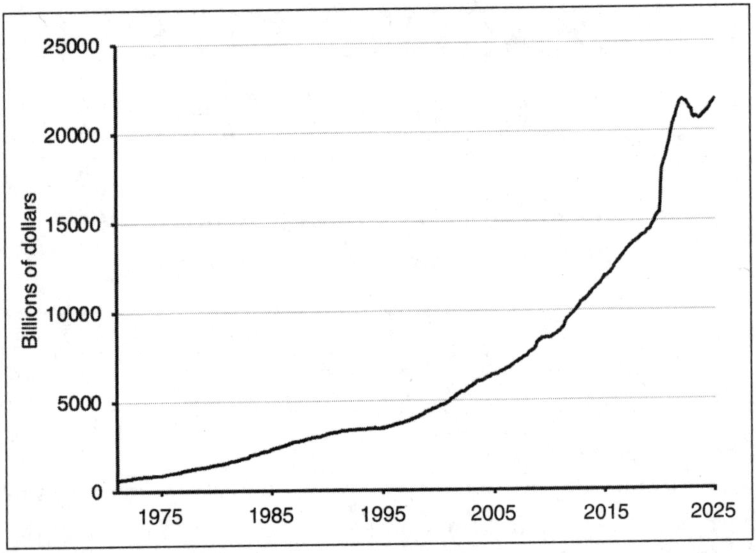

Source: Board of Governors of the Federal Reserve System (U.S.) via FRED.

*Roughly 40% of all U.S. dollars now in circulation were created in those few short pandemic years.*

To be fair, decision-makers were facing an unprecedented crisis. Maybe they fully understood the long-term inflationary consequences, and maybe they didn't. In that moment, they had to choose between higher prices later, or people going hungry and losing their homes *now*. The truth is probably messy and multifaceted: they, too, were at the mercy of the system already in place. Some may have acted out of urgency, others out of ideology, and some, perhaps, out of genuine ignorance.

→»

But here's what most people don't realize, and what the chart so clearly shows: the money supply had already been growing steadily for decades. Even before Covid, M2 had been expanding at an average rate of nearly 7% per year,[24] quietly adding water to the wine. What happened in 2020 wasn't the beginning of the problem. It was, rather, the dramatic acceleration of a long-running pattern.

Money supply matters because, as we saw in the last chapter with the trading cards, every newly added dollar erodes the purchasing power of the dollars already in your wallet.

So if your income and assets aren't outpacing that monetary expansion, you're essentially losing in real terms, year after year.

Think of it this way: if the money supply is swelling at roughly 7% a year while your salary climbs only 3%, your "real" paycheck is actually shrinking—in terms of buying power—about 4% annually.

So who gets the wine, and who's left with the water?

→»

Perhaps nowhere in our lives is the impact of this phenomenon more unmistakable than in the cost of that central pillar of the American Dream: home ownership.

As the money supply grows, it seeks shelter in hard assets that'll preserve and grow in value, and real estate is often the first in line.

Home prices balloon, and paychecks don't keep pace. The effect is catastrophic.

Whether it's longtime renters watching homeownership slip further out of reach, middle-class families struggling to make payments amidst the rising costs of everything else, or retirees on a fixed income worried that their savings won't even cover modest expenses and property taxes, soaring home prices have made life harder for almost all of us.

And for young people just starting out—those who followed all the rules, earned good degrees, landed solid jobs, and worked hard to build strong credit—the dream of homeownership has slipped almost entirely out of reach.[25]

↦

Tragically, this economic reality is also forcing millennials and Generation Z to confront a deeply personal and emotional decision: delaying having children because salaries simply can't keep up with the rising cost of living. In 2020, the U.S. birth rate was lower than it had been at any point in history. As *The Wall Street Journal* put it, "Even before the pandemic taught us to expect the unexpected, members of the millennial generation often considered postponing having children until they achieved financial milestones."[26]

I can relate to these studies, because as much as I've always wanted to start my own family, I, too, have consistently put off that chapter of my life. Seeing the toll that financial hardship can take on people, especially children—through years of reporting and in my own parents' struggles—I felt I had no choice but to keep working toward financial stability before I could focus on building a family of my own.

↦

It didn't used to be this way. Let's take a look at the situation back in 1971—a truly pivotal year—to see how much things have changed.

Back in 1971, you might recall from Figure 1 in the first chapter, the median home price in the U.S. was about $25,800, while the median household income was around $10,300, representing a home-to-income ratio of roughly 2.5x. This meant that even a single-income household on a modest salary, like that of a post office worker or teacher, could reasonably afford a home.

Fast forward to 2025, the median home price has soared to more than $410,000, while the median household income is about $80,600. That's a home-to-income ratio of more than 5x, making homeownership twice as unaffordable compared to 50 years ago.

→»

To make matters worse, the burden of monthly mortgage payments has also grown substantially since then. As home prices spiked over the past two decades, even modest increases in interest rates would have made mortgages unaffordable for many families, let alone the aggressive hikes we've actually seen.

In fact, between 2019 and 2024, mortgage payments more than doubled,[27] adding to the difficulties of homeownership.

It bears repeating: for nearly 50% of Americans today, the dream of buying a home now seems entirely unattainable. Wages haven't kept pace, costs have skyrocketed, and our dollars continue to lose purchasing power. Chances are, you've already felt the impact.

We're not crazy. We really can't square the circle.

→»

As noted earlier, we've been adding water to the wine—at a rate of 7% or so—for decades! A few drops might've been manageable, especially if wages *had* kept up with the expanding money supply.

But again, the data clearly reveals that they haven't. And we know this in our bones, data notwithstanding: none of my employers have ever given me a 7% annual raise! Have yours?

And yet, prices keep climbing: not necessarily because the things we're buying have improved, but because our dollars have weakened.

Take older homes, for example. For the most part, they haven't suddenly become more spacious, better built, or retrofitted with cutting-edge appliances. They've grown more expensive primarily because there's more money in circulation competing for them. And, adding insult to injury, institutions—who are able to access the new money first—have been gobbling up real estate at breakneck speed. They've done so not just to profit from renters who can no longer afford to buy, but because real estate is one of the few assets that holds and increases its value in an inflationary system.

*That's* why the house that hasn't been renovated since 1970 now costs an astonishing half a million dollars. The wine glass isn't just being diluted, it's practically overflowing with wine-flavored water.

At its core, a home's worth should come from what it provides us: a place to raise a family and build a life. These days, however, homes are treated as much like investments as they are places to live, with rising prices often celebrated as a sign of prosperity and evidence of financial security and smart investment.

For many homeowners, that "gain" masks a more complicated reality: while the price of properties in some regions has soared, the money supply has actually expanded even faster, outpacing the appreciation of most homes. Higher home values also bring higher taxes, bigger insurance premiums, and steeper maintenance costs. Selling may unlock a windfall—but unless they're leaving their region entirely, homeowners are often just recycling that equity into another inflated home.

At the same time, affluent investors—including large institutions—continue to buy up multiple properties—not to live in, but where they can *park money, collect rent, and wait for their assets to appreciate.* In doing so, they drive up prices and push hardworking families out.

What was once the cornerstone of the American Dream has become a game that fewer and fewer people can afford to play.

→»

And it's not just the real estate market, either. Again: when the money supply expands, the prices of other assets, like stocks, also go up. At first glance, this might look like economic growth or wealth creation. But in many cases, stock value mirrors those illusory home-value increases: it just *looks* like financial progress. Company shares aren't necessarily rising because of real value being created, they're often just riding the same wave of inflation that distorts everything else.

That's a sobering truth: those "gains" we see in the housing *and* stock market aren't necessarily signs of real prosperity. For many who own a home or have a retirement account, it may look like they're doing well on paper. And yes, they're certainly faring better than the average wage earner, who struggles just to break even. But even in that "better" scenario, most people are simply keeping pace with the expanding money supply—not actually building wealth.

In more ways than we often realize, the actual "best case" scenario is reserved for the *truly* wealthy.

As we've touched on, the wealthy and well-connected enjoy early and privileged access to newly created money. They can borrow unfathomable sums to buy *even more* assets using leverage, often for next to nothing.

This isn't about a few bad actors gaming the system. It's about the system itself: legal but profoundly skewed, quietly extracting from those with the least and funneling wealth upward to those with the most. And because much of this happens behind a maze of financial complexity, most of us don't notice what's really going on.

In the chapters ahead, we'll unpack how this machinery works, and why it's been so difficult to see until now.

↦

To make sense of one of the most crucial—and least understood—aspects of this financial maze, let's turn to one of the most iconic board games of all time: Monopoly.

Imagine you've carved out a couple of hours to play Monopoly with some friends. The game starts as it always does: with a clear set of rules and a *fixed supply of money*.

Everyone strategizes based on the resources available, and the game progresses predictably: people collect money as they pass "Go!", buy up properties, and build houses and hotels in order to collect rent and generate income.

However, halfway through the game, the banker suddenly doubles the amount of available money. And instead of distributing this new wealth equally among all players, *the banker rewards those who've already acquired the most properties in the game*. This, quite obviously, creates a sudden and significant wealth disparity.

↦

The players with the new influx of cash were already winning; now they have *even more* buying power and can therefore buy up *even more* properties on each turn.

"But the cards still say $400 for Boardwalk," you protest. True. But the moment two cash-rich players both want the same property, the printed price becomes little more than the opening bid. Players can (and will!) offer far above face value.

By adding new money to the game, as this illustration shows, the banker has created a situation in which **more money is chasing the same number of properties, effectively reducing the purchasing power of every dollar that was already in circulation**. The prices of all properties—and especially the most desirable ones—go up.

**Figure 3: Dollars chasing homes**

Players with no connection to this "new money pipeline" are in the dark about the doubled money supply and are therefore at a huge disadvantage. Their chances of winning are drastically reduced: no matter what they do, it has become pretty much structurally impossible for them to catch up.

Naturally, there will always be winners and losers in a normal round of Monopoly. But for the game to work—and to be any fun, for that matter—*the same rules must apply to everyone*. It would be absurd for the banker to give extra money to certain players. But believe it or not, this is precisely what happens out here in the real world.

Out here, the rules of the game depend on where you're sitting.

⇥

It's this flood of new money—and the wealth concentration that results—that brings us to the bold idea at the heart of Bitcoin and of this book:

**Money that can be inflated cannot hold its value. Money that is immune to inflation preserves and builds wealth.**

To understand why, let's return to our wine metaphor. Wine doesn't just come from nowhere, of course—someone has to grow the grapes, harvest them, and go through a careful process to transform them into a product of far greater complexity and appeal.

In the same way, no matter what form it takes—dollars, euros, yuan, or any of the 150+ national currencies—money represents the time, energy, and effort we trade to earn it. We work hard to "fill our glass," trusting it won't get watered down.

But when someone comes along and undermines that trust, everything changes. The fruits of our efforts are diluted.

It may feel like this is just the nature of "how economies work," but that's mostly because we were never taught how it *really* works. In reality, there's a powerful mechanism pumping out that dilutionary new money: it's known as the *money printer*, and it affects every corner of our economy.

⇥

# Chapter 3 Summary

Most people think inflation just means rising prices, but that's only part of the story. This chapter goes deeper, revealing how inflation is driven by the quiet expansion of the money supply. We point to the fact that newly created money doesn't flow evenly through the economy—it reaches asset markets like real estate and stocks long before it reaches paychecks, a topic we will explore in greater depth in the coming chapters. As a result, wages lag while home prices, living costs, and inequality surge. Through the example of Monopoly, we show how this hidden mechanism distorts the economy and erodes everyday wealth.

**Key Takeaway**: Inflation isn't just an economic side effect; it's a feature of the system. And unless your income and assets grow faster than the money supply, you're probably losing ground without even realizing it.

# 4.
# EVERYONE'S AFFECTED BY THE MONEY PRINTER

"Show me the incentive, and I'll
show you the outcome."

CHARLIE MUNGER

---

WHEN YOU HEAR "money printer," you might envision old-school newsreels showing sheets of paper bills pouring out of giant printing machines.

However, modern money creation rarely involves any printing at all—it's far more subtle and complex. Most of the money in our economy is created digitally, through an opaque mechanism involving the relationship between *central banks* and the broader banking system.

Chapter Five explores the reasons for money printing in greater depth. For now, we'll take a look at how this little-known process actually works, and how it quietly chips away at our ability to save, invest, and build real wealth.

—

Of course, it's not as simple as a banker tossing fistfuls of cash around a Monopoly board. But the reality isn't as far off as you may think.

To understand the way new money *really* enters the picture, we need to take a look at the *Federal Reserve*—the central bank of the United States—and its relationship with both the U.S. Treasury and the commercial banking sector.

Though the actions are complex and often difficult to interpret, this dynamic has a direct effect on our overall money supply. So let's dive in and explore it.

—

The Federal Reserve (or "the Fed," as it's known) is made up of 12 regional banks, located in New York, Boston, Philadelphia, Cleveland, Richmond, Atlanta, Chicago, St. Louis, Minneapolis, Kansas City, Dallas, and San Francisco.

It was intended (at least on paper), "to provide the nation with a safer, more flexible, and more stable monetary and financial system."[28] Overseen by an *unelected* Fed Chair and an *unelected* Board of Governors nominated by the President and approved by the Senate, the Fed's not quite private and not quite public.

The central bank sits at the apex of America's banking system, closely followed by the banks you'll recognize as some of the most prominent financial institutions in the United States—household names like JPMorgan Chase, Citibank, Bank of America, and Morgan Stanley.

These banks keep their own accounts at the Federal Reserve, much like the checking account you keep at your local bank.

The Fed and these commercial banks have a unique, symbiotic relationship—almost resembling, as we shall see, a co-dependent partnership.

**Figure 4: U.S. banking system**

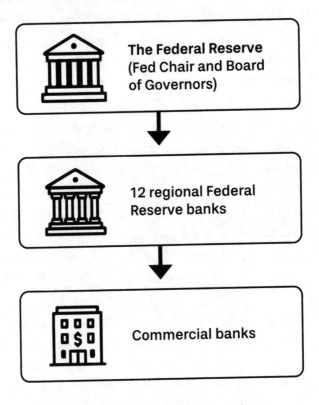

No matter which party runs Washington, the federal government habitually spends more than it collects in taxes. To cover the gap, the Treasury borrows the funds by selling *interest-bearing bonds*, which are essentially IOUs.

Here's a quick Treasury bond 101: When someone buys a bond, they're lending money to the government. In return, the government promises to pay it back later, with interest.

Let's say you buy a 10-year Treasury bond for $1,000 with an interest rate of 4%. Each year, the government will send you $40 in interest (4% of $1,000 is $40), and at the end of 10 years (when the bond matures), you'll get your original $1,000 back plus you will have received the $400 you've accumulated through those interest payments.

Because they're backed by the "full faith and credit of the U.S. government," Treasury bonds—or, simply, "Treasuries"—have been among the most trusted assets in the world for the last century.

⇥

Who buys these bonds? All kinds of people, including institutions, retirement funds, foreign governments, and individual investors.

However, and most importantly for our discussion, the big commercial banks are *required* to do so, ensuring the government can always find buyers for its debt. And since they must participate in Treasury auctions, the big banks are known as *primary dealers*.

Ordinarily, these banks and other buyers use their existing funds or reserves to purchase Treasury bonds. The money they spend then goes into the Treasury's account at the Federal Reserve, allowing the government to fund its operations. In this case, money is moved from the private sector to the government, but no new money is created.

**But when there aren't enough buyers for all that debt, the central bank can step in and fire up the money printer to ensure buyers for the government's bonds.**

⇥

This is *monetary inflation* in action: rather than drawing from existing reserves or a savings account, the government can rely on the central bank to make adjustments that fill the gap.

Today, Washington borrows trillions just to cover yesterday's interest. It's like paying your Visa bill with a brand-new Mastercard. Only a government with its own money printer can keep that game alive seemingly indefinitely.

As we will see, these actions ultimately pump new money through the system and amount to the *money printing* that's as skewed towards the "haves" in our own society as the Monopoly banker's new-cash handouts were to the existing property owners in that hypothetical game.

Over time, money printing makes everything more expensive for all of us. **In essence, we are trading our (very real!) time for something that others can create out of thin air**.

And it doesn't end there. For reasons we'll explore in the coming chapters, those ultra-safe U.S. bonds don't just anchor the U.S. economy: *they underpin the entire global financial system*.

→»

So we know that the Fed, commercial banks, and the U.S. Treasury are the players; now it's time to take a look at the game.

Money creation is a tag-team effort: the Fed supplies fresh dollars, banks multiply them into new deposits through lending, and interest-rate policy controls the pace of the entire routine. The next pages unpack each step.

→»

# How the Fed creates fresh dollars from thin air

The Fed has two official mandates—price stability and maximum employment—but it also quietly serves an unofficial third: keeping the Treasury market liquid. Because if that multi-hundred-trillion-dollar backbone of finance stalls, every other priority (and the broader economy) would falter, too.

If private investors aren't buying enough Treasuries, the Fed can step in. It doesn't dig into a vault or call another central bank for a loan—instead, a Fed official opens a computer and *types a bigger number into the reserve account of a commercial bank.*

Those keystrokes create brand-new digital dollars on the spot.

In exchange, the Fed takes some of the bank's Treasury bonds onto its books, essentially buying back bonds that the banks had legitimately paid for, with money the Fed produced out of nowhere. The banks walk away with fresh cash to lend or invest, bond prices stay steady, and the whole system keeps humming. No new tax dollars need to be raised, just a few keystrokes at the Fed.

You read that right.

*The Federal Reserve can literally change the numbers on the banks' balance sheets, effectively creating new money out of thin air.*

This maneuver, known as quantitative easing or "QE" for short, reached unprecedented levels during the pandemic response. It was directly responsible for that massive increase in our money supply.

Whenever financial markets wobble, economic growth slows, or crises emerge, this mechanism is activated. It bears repeating: nearly 40% of all U.S. dollars in existence today were created after the Covid-19 pandemic.

These newly created dollars weren't the product of hard work, innovation, or productivity—they simply materialized at the press of a button and were then funneled into the system.

"Here you go," the Fed essentially tells the commercial banks in its network. "We've added new dollars to your balance sheet and used that cash to take those old bonds off your hands. Have at it!"

It really is as simple as that. As Christopher Leonard, author of *The Lords of Easy Money*, describes it:

> A trader at the New York Fed would call up one of the primary dealers, like JPMorgan Chase and offer to buy $8 billion worth of Treasury bonds from the bank. JPMorgan would sell the Treasury bonds to the Fed trader. Then the Fed trader would hit a few keys and tell the Morgan banker to look inside the reserve account. Voila, the Fed had instantly created $8 billion out of thin air, in the reserve account, to complete the purchase. Morgan could, in turn, use this money to buy assets in the wider marketplace. This is how the Fed creates money—it buys things from the primary dealers, and it does so by simply creating money inside their reserve accounts.[29]

It's a great deal for the government and banks. The government has instant guaranteed buyers for its debt (driving up demand overall and pushing down interest rates), and the banks become flush with extra cash with which to buy even *more* bonds and issue *more* loans.

Which brings us to:

⇻⟩⟩

# How banks use ordinary loans to create a new wave of money ("Fractional Reserve Lending")

It would be bad enough if the story ended there: big banks close to the Fed getting free money to buy government bonds, while everyone else's money lost value. But it *doesn't* end there.

Banks use this special privilege to multiply money even further through everyday loans.

Imagine you're taking out a $250,000 mortgage to buy a home. You might assume that banks lend this money directly from their reserves, the way a friend would be down $20 if they loaned that $20 to you. But that's not really how it works. Instead, banks simply credit your account with $250,000 (without debiting that amount from anywhere!) while holding only a small fraction of that amount in their reserves.

This is called *fractional reserve lending*, an important concept we will explore more deeply in later chapters. **With each loan, it turns out, money isn't transferred—it's** *created*.

→»

Here's the kicker: the bank only needs about $25,000 (typically 10%) in reserves to issue that $250,000 loan. And where do those reserves predominantly come from? *Straight from the Fed's money printer.*

This cycle repeats and repeats. Each round of lending multiplies the total supply of money circulating in the economy, accelerating the dilution of value like water in our wine glass. This phenomenon is known as the *multiplier effect*, and it massively amplifies the impact of the Fed's initial money creation.

As reserves turn into new loans, and those loans create even more money (and even more loans!), the cycle continues to feed on itself.

Most of us, like those unlucky Monopoly players, end up *literally* paying the price.

And yet, this entire chain reaction is still at the mercy of yet another powerful force. While this "third tool" doesn't create money directly, it nevertheless profoundly influences the flow of money through our economy: *interest rates*. Interest rates serve as a kind of spigot for the entire system, directly affecting the speed and impact of inflation.

⇻

## How interest rates hit the gas (or slam the brakes) on money printing

The Fed sets the "price of money" via the interest rate by making borrowing either cheaper or more expensive.

When the Fed lowers the interest rate, banks pay less to borrow cash and lend more the next day. New loans put extra dollars into circulation, nudging mortgage, car-loan, and credit-card rates lower as well. Raise the target and the opposite happens: borrowing costs more, banks pull back on lending, and the flow of new money slows, cooling the economy but also dampening growth.

Bottom line: by turning this rate knob up or down, the Fed doesn't inject money directly into the economy, but it strongly encourages banks and borrowers to create (or hold back) money through lending—much like opening or closing a valve on a water pipe.

This ability to indirectly expand or contract the money supply through interest rates is one of the Fed's most important tools for steering the economy.

⇻

And now, we've finally come to the point where we can unpack a dynamic we've been building towards throughout the last few chapters. Like the extra bills handed by the Monopoly banker to the game's front-runners, **all of this new money reaches society's "haves" first**. The asset owners and Wall Street traders quickly begin to bid up stocks and real estate; later, it ripples into everyday prices, leaving the rest of us struggling to keep up with the consequences of dollars manufactured from thin air.

**Figure 5: Where printed money goes**

Here's another way to visualize it.

Imagine our financial system as a terraced mountain. The Federal Reserve "money printer" is perched at the top, with the power to unleash fresh dollars at the press of a button. These dollars flow directly to the cluster of big banks sitting just below the peak, which quickly lend those new dollars, in turn, to their own best customers (big corporations, Wall Street firms, and high net worth individuals), allowing *them* to snap up assets like stocks, bonds, and other businesses.

Down on the next ledge, where families and small businesses live—like your favorite Mom-and-Pop sandwich shop—the stream has diminished significantly. The dollars still reach these folks, but their purchasing power has already eroded due to the rising prices triggered by the activity up top. They can't compete with large corporations that have deeper pockets and lower risk in the eyes of bankers, the ones who first received the printed money and spent it *before* prices rose.

By the time it reaches the base of the mountain—the lowest-income households—only traces of that monetary surge remain. Everything costs more, while wages continue to lag.

**Figure 6: Money printer mountain**

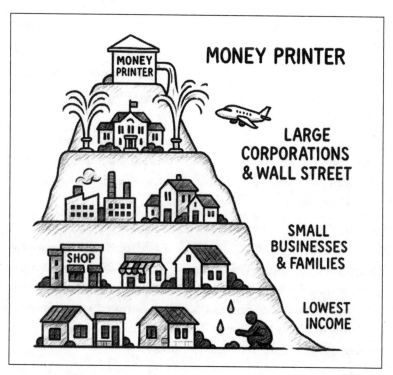

This is what happens in our financial system when new money is created and distributed unevenly: if it feels like you're falling behind, it's because you are.

→»

Economists call this phenomenon the *Cantillon Effect*: those closest to the money printer get first access and use the new money to buy valuable assets *before* prices rise, leaving everyone else down the line to deal with the fallout.

It isn't just infuriating and unfair. It's a structural feature of the system Carl Icahn was talking about, where **the rich keep getting richer in an endless feedback loop of wealth concentration.**

→»

Money creation has become a regular practice over the past few decades.

As Leonard summarized it, "The Federal Reserve's one superpower is its ability to create new dollars and pump them into the banking system."[30]

**At the end of the day, this is the *hidden tax* of monetary inflation. The banks get the money, but we eventually pay for it—at the checkout counter, in our monthly rent, and in the fading dream of owning a home.**

This "tax" isn't debated publicly, in Congress, or voted on, and isn't listed on a paycheck, like deductions for Social Security or unemployment. But if a tax is money we're required to give to the government, then this uninvited burden fits the bill precisely: we have no choice but to absorb the costs associated with financing government spending through monetary inflation. Though indirect, our contributions are undeniably compulsory.

→»

Here's the thing. Yes, new money *does* stimulate actual economic activity. Homes get built, cars get sold. However, the production of new goods takes *time*, whereas printing money is virtually *instantaneous*.

At any given moment, there's only so much land, food, housing, and raw material to go around. **You can create more money with the stroke of a key, but that doesn't mean that more homes will instantly materialize.** As we've seen, when the supply of available money grows, but the supply of real things remains at least temporarily limited—like Monopoly properties—those things get more expensive.

## Breakout explanation: private equity

One area where these dynamics are especially visible is in private equity (PE). PE firms—investment groups that buy entire companies in a manner similar to purchasing shares of a public company—often use debt to finance their acquisitions. They may acquire a business using borrowed funds, then place that debt on the company's books. In some cases, they also purchase the company's real estate and lease it back to the business.

Afterwards, PE owners often seek to boost short-term profitability through cost reductions such as staff cuts, scaled-back inventory, and deferred maintenance. If the company is later sold, its assets—such as property, brand rights, or equipment—may be part of the exit strategy, with the owners paying themselves dividends along the way.

One high-profile example is Toys "R" Us. In 2005, three major PE firms took the retailer private in a $6.6 billion leveraged buyout, with about $5 billion financed through debt. The company faced substantial interest payments, reduced staffing, and fewer store upgrades, while its new owners collected fees and dividends. By 2017, Toys "R" Us filed for bankruptcy, closed hundreds of stores, and laid off tens of thousands of employees. Though the brand still exists under new ownership, the PE-led restructuring left behind shuttered storefronts, displaced workers, and communities dealing with the aftermath; reminders of the lasting impact of debt-driven takeovers.

**Bottom line: the abundance of money creates scarcity everywhere else.**

⇢

Our entire economy has become wildly distorted. We've been stuck in a Monopoly game that has long since abandoned the rules. The engine that fuels our modern monetary system runs on rising debt and relentless growth, and—like any engine that runs too hot—it often risks overheating.

Debt was once used judiciously to spur growth; now it's a matter of survival. Both as individuals and as a society, we can no longer function without borrowing. We exhaust our credit cards, kicking the consequences down the road and hoping for the best: as of this writing, U.S. credit card debt stands at record levels and shows no sign of slowing.

Similarly, at the top of the mountain and on a grand (and almost incomprehensible) scale, money printing has turned into a *requirement* for economic functioning.

⇢

Like any stimulant, there's no doubt that injecting new money into the domestic bloodstream spurs real productivity: again, as it slowly makes its way through the economy, housing developments spring up, bridges can be built, and companies formed.

Unfortunately this stimulant behaves a lot like a habit-forming drug: escalating doses are eventually needed to achieve the same results.

The now-universal economic system that emerged from our dependence on money printing has created extraordinarily rapid growth for decades. But like any addiction, it has come at a cost.

What's more, it's working against the very forces that should be making life easier. As tech entrepreneur Jeff Booth points out, advances in technology naturally make things cheaper—we get more for less, which should improve everyone's standard of living.

But a system built on debt can't survive falling prices. So instead of embracing this deflationary gift, we must double down on debt to keep inflation going.

→»

Today, our fortunes are largely determined by how close—or how far away—we are from the money printer, not by our skill, efforts, or value we contribute to society.

And history clearly suggests that when the game starts to seem unwinnable, societal instability usually isn't far behind. A quote widely attributed to Henry Ford states, "It is well enough that people of the nation do not understand our banking and monetary system, for if they did, I believe there would be a revolution before tomorrow morning."

When protesters rail against capitalism and oligarchy, they are responding not to the impacts of "capitalism," per se, but rather to the symptoms of a system warped by broken money. Our economy is a tangle of cheap debt, back-room deals, and money summoned at a keystroke for the benefit of insiders.

→»

Thankfully, ignorance and revolution aren't our only two choices. When we once again tie new investment to real saving and honest risk, many of these problems will begin to self-correct. To truly understand how Bitcoin—a decentralized system of "rules without rulers"—fixes the money and restores our ability to save and flourish without interference, we first need to go back to the beginning.

We need to understand what money really is.

→»

# Chapter 4 Summary

Money printing refers to digital dollars created by the Federal Reserve and funneled into the banking system, and then into the economy through loans and asset purchases. But this process benefits those closest to the source—banks, corporations, and wealthy investors—who can use the new money before prices rise.

The rest of us experience the fallout: higher costs for homes, goods, and services without a proportional increase in income. This isn't an accident—it's a built-in feature of the system, often referred to as the Cantillon Effect. Money printing quietly shifts wealth upward while eroding the value of our savings and wages.

This structural feature of modern monetary policy has become a permanent fixture of our economy, distorting incentives and fostering dependence on cheap debt. Meanwhile, the tools of real growth—saving, investment, and entrepreneurship—are increasingly sidelined.

**Key Takeaway**: The modern money system redistributes wealth from the many to the few. Those nearest the source of new money gain first—and everyone else is left paying the hidden tax of inflation.

# 5.
# EVERYONE
# NEEDS MONEY

**"Gold is money. Everything else is credit."**

J.P. MORGAN

---

**M**ONEY ISN'T JUST about what's in our bank account, of course—it's also the driving force behind much of human history. To study money is to study humanity itself: the rise and fall of empires, the ebb and flow of economies, and the power struggles behind all of it.

↦

Over time, money has come to serve three distinct functions:

1. As a *medium of exchange*, it helps us buy and sell things without barter.

2. As a *unit of account*, it provides a standardized way to price things.

3. As a *store of value*, it enables us to save for the future.

While currency—the physical and digital forms of money we use every day—functions well as a medium of exchange, it has largely failed as a store of value. A dollar might easily buy you a coffee today, but saving that dollar for years won't preserve its purchasing power: you'll need more dollars to buy that same coffee in the future. Instead of *holding* value over time, our currency gradually *loses* it, leaving us with less and less in real terms.

In this book, we're focusing primarily on money's function as a store of value, which I view as the most important use case for Bitcoin.

–»

When I was growing up, my immigrant parents—who came from Poland, where investing wasn't an option—made it clear to my brother and me that saving money was a form of protection against an uncertain future. Under communism, the means of production were controlled by the government and everyone earned just enough to get by; the system was designed to ensure that people lived day to day, unable to accumulate wealth and therefore "get ahead."

In such a difficult political and economic environment, people had to find clever and often dangerous workarounds to build at least a degree of financial security.

–»

That early lesson has stayed with me. Studying money has led me to think of saving as a sort of financial battery: we store the fruits of our labor (our *work*) in a way that preserves its value for future use. Just as batteries hold energy until we need it, so should money *retain the economic energy* (value) we've generated until we're ready to spend it.

*Should.*

As we saw in earlier chapters, inflation has thwarted our ability to build wealth through hard work and frugality alone. To even tread water now, we must invest.

-»»

Inflation drains money of its value over time, incentivizing us to spend as soon as possible, when money's worth as much as it'll ever be. Disciplining ourselves to forgo consumption in the short term would only make sense if our money was to *keep* or even *increase* its value in the long run.

Many of us feel quiet shame about our inability to save, but we shouldn't: there are enormous forces at play that make saving money not only impossible, but positively *irrational*.

It's not us. It's the money.

-»»

In terms of their ability to store value, the breathtaking array of objects that have been used as money throughout history have delivered mixed results.

To explore these artifacts is not only to gain tremendous insights into the priorities and values of cultures across the globe—their unique geographies, needs, rituals, and forms of hierarchy and governance—but also to begin to understand the essential *properties* of money itself.

You name it: shells, beads, salt, and even teeth[31] have been used as money.

Money whose supply can be expanded relatively easily and thus tends to lose value over time—like beads, shells, or salt—is known as *easy money*. Sound familiar?

On the other hand, money that's significantly more difficult to produce and which tends to preserve (or even increase) its value over time—like silver and gold—is known as *hard money*.

Throughout history, gold (and then the dollar backed by gold) has been the reigning champion of hard money—but pretty soon, you'll meet the challenger poised to claim the title.

$$\twoheadrightarrow$$

Gold emerged thousands of years ago as the global winner for storing value, serving as a medium of exchange, and ultimately becoming the benchmark for monetary systems everywhere. To understand why, let's briefly explore the specific properties of hard money.

One important quality of "good money" is *durability*, which we can define as its ability to last over time. For obvious reasons, it wouldn't work to have money that rots, rusts, or otherwise degrades. Gold is pretty much indestructible.

Good money is also *fungible* and *divisible*. "Fungible" means that the units of money are completely interchangeable, like standardized coins. Every nickel is the same as every other nickel. We also need money to make purchases ranging from houses and cars to books and candy bars; gold can be melted and shaped into bars or coins of various values and traded accordingly.

Good money should be *portable*. This is a big one, and it's had a major impact upon the evolution of our global financial system. Gold is, indeed, highly portable in small amounts: you probably picture, as I often do, people in the Middle Ages trading pouches of gold coins tied with a drawstring, or Ebenezer Scrooge greedily counting his pile. But in larger quantities, gold is extremely costly to transport due to its heavy weight and the security needed to protect it, making long-distance trade and large transactions impractical and expensive.

Good money must also be *salable*, which essentially means "exchangeable." Salability is the measurement of how easy it is to sell or exchange. Throughout time and around the world, there have always been buyers for gold—this high salability is, indeed, one of gold's strongest attributes.

Finally, good money is *scarce*. I've saved this one for last because it's really important. It points both to the key problems of broken money and, as we'll see, a central feature of Bitcoin.

Gold, for instance, has maintained its status as a reliable store of value partly because of its natural scarcity. Even if demand increases, obtaining more gold is difficult and slow due to the physical, environmental, and logistical challenges of mining. As a result, gold's annual inflation rate (the rate at which the total gold supply expands) remains steady at around 1.5–2% per year, regardless of fluctuations in demand.

**Table 3: The six properties of good (hard) money**

| Durability | Portability | Fungibility |
|---|---|---|
| Salability | Scarcity | Divisibility |

⇻

Now that we've established the prerequisites of good money, let's take a step back and examine the damage that can be done when money *doesn't* fulfill those requirements.

Long before gold rose to dominance as the world's hardest money, humans used other forms of money, including those shells, beads, and teeth mentioned earlier. Like gold, these items didn't rot, they were portable (often woven into clothing or jewelry, they could be carried easily, even across long distances), and—while no two are *exactly* alike—they were relatively uniform in terms of size and weight. People could pay each other for items of varying value using a greater or lesser number of shells or teeth, which were widely desirable to most cultures and thus easily traded.

But most importantly, they were also typically quite *scarce*—until, as the following cautionary tale illustrates, they weren't.

↦

In *The Bitcoin Standard*, Saifedean Ammous points out that, for centuries, the people of western Africa found "aggry beads"—small, decorative glass beads—to be a useful form of money.[32]

The system worked nicely until the arrival of European explorers and traders in the 16th century[33] who quickly identified an opportunity: with their advanced technology, the Europeans were able to produce large quantities of such beads at low cost, and use them to trade for goods and resources in Africa. At first, nobody noticed the influx of "new money" entering the African economy; people simply continued to trade for these prized beads.

Eventually, though, there were so many beads flooding the market that their value plummeted. They'd been a form of "good money" for a long while, but as soon as their supply was dramatically inflated, the beads degraded into easy money: they were everywhere, and thus much less valuable.

If this was simply an unfortunate fate for an established system of money, it would be perhaps no more than academically interesting. But because the Europeans were able to take control of—and expand—the supply of money itself, they effectively transferred ownership of African wealth away from its citizens and into European hands.

**"Printing" more aggry beads led directly to the extraction of Africa's abundant resources from its own people.**

All over the world, people's ability (or lack thereof) to store their work in a form of money that can't be debased has profoundly affected their lives and, indeed, shaped the course of history.

If the supply of a form of money can be increased—either through discovering a new source or through the ability to mechanically reproduce it—it is a very poor *store of value*. Someone will always be incentivized to mine, manufacture, or *print* it, and then use that capacity to acquire resources, leaving a degraded form of money in its wake.

*Are you starting to see the pattern?*

↦

Now that we can clearly recognize why the only true protection against the threat of monetary debasement is the hardest money a society can find, we can more closely examine why—until now—gold emerged as the undisputed winner for most of human history.

Unlike glass beads or other items once used as money, no matter how advanced our technology has become, humans haven't figured out a way to artificially produce gold. Remarkably, by the early 20th century, all the gold ever mined would fit into a "modest two-story townhouse."[34]

It's also important to note that gold didn't become a form of money because it was imposed by those in power; it emerged because the market recognized its universally valued qualities. These benefits were further enhanced with the introduction of coins, as early as the 6th century BC, which eliminated the need to weigh raw gold for every trade. Coins could also be stamped with a government seal to provide authenticity and added credibility.

Coins are largely considered an unnecessary nuisance these days (have you ever noticed a penny on the street and decided that it wasn't worth the effort to bend down and pick it up?), but they're also a fascinating artifact of the evolution of money.

↦

With the development of coins, though, came an irresistible temptation for those in power.

If you have any loose change, try running your fingernail along the edge. Feel the ridges?

You've probably noticed them without stopping to question why they're there. Those ridges were originally designed (by none other than Sir Isaac Newton[35]) to prevent *coin clipping*—the practice of shaving small amounts off the edges of gold coins or diluting them with cheaper metals. In the U.S., this design feature is a relic from the days when coins were actually made of precious metals like silver and copper.

Coin clipping was once a discreet way for the powerful to accumulate wealth. The logic is simple: if a king knows his subjects would revolt against higher taxes to fund a war but wouldn't notice the gradual reduction of precious metals in their coins (currency debasement, or monetary inflation), the choice is clear—he'd opt for debasement almost every time.

Take the Roman emperor Nero, for example: he reduced the weight of the *denarius*—the standard coin at the time—by replacing precious metals with cheaper alloys. Whether he was driven by financial pressures or self-interest, we may never know.

What matters is what the example here reveals: whenever a currency can be debased, leaders almost always find a reason to do so.

↦

Thus the seeds of inflation are sown, and with them a loss of trust among citizens and trade partners alike. The devaluation of currency has weakened economies and diminished the authority of rulers throughout history, and has, indeed, played a significant role in the decline of mighty empires and global powers.

The process of debasement can take years (or even decades) to ripple through an economy. But just like the mass-produced beads that flooded African markets, an inflated currency will inevitably diminish in value. At this point, we know all too well—having explored the process and implications of money printing in prior chapters (and likely experienced its effects firsthand)—that people's savings and purchasing power eroded right along with it.[36]

As we'll see in Chapter Fourteen, however, it can also happen overnight: people can go to bed with $1,000 in the bank and wake up to find that it only purchases $500 worth of goods. This kind of silent theft naturally breeds frustration and resentment, fueling civil unrest and political instability.

Throughout history, when populations find themselves trapped in an unwinnable race against devaluation, they don't just get angry— they demand change.

→»

Coin clipping and debasement eroded trust in many early currencies minted from the precious metal. But gold itself remained largely resilient.

Its durability and scarcity ensured that it retained its status as a reliable store of value and a cornerstone of economic stability, ultimately leading to the establishment of the global *gold standard* in the 19th and early 20th centuries. This was a pivotal moment in monetary history.

By providing countries with a universal unit of account and eliminating the need to navigate disparate currencies, the gold standard would help fuel a boom in international trade and investment. It would also play a crucial role in the ascendance of the United States as a financial powerhouse.

↦

**Yet, despite its strengths, gold has a natural Achilles heel: its physicality.**

Gold's qualities may have made it an ideal store of value, but its sheer bulk posed serious challenges as economies expanded. Transporting and storing large quantities of gold across oceans or over vast, treacherous landscapes was both risky and impractical. This made settling large gold transactions slow and cumbersome— adding delays and frictions that rendered day-to-day use nearly impossible.

Gold's weight and lack of portability made it vulnerable, leading to a reliance on centralized institutions and intermediaries to manage and secure it.

This vulnerability would ultimately change the course of history.

↦

# Chapter 5 Summary

---

Money has three primary functions: it serves as a medium of exchange, a unit of account, and a store of value. The dollar does a fine job with the first two, but it does not preserve its value over time. Societies have used many forms of money throughout history. The "hardest" money (a money supply that's difficult to produce, like gold) has always triumphed.

Gold has been the undisputed winner for centuries because it possesses certain essential properties.

Scarcity is crucial: whenever that scarcity has been somehow compromised (through debasement or the ability to mass produce more of that money), ordinary people have suffered. Gold's physical nature, however—its lack of portability—presented a critical vulnerability that would ultimately reshape monetary systems worldwide.

**Key Takeaway**: Sound money must be scarce. When money can be easily created, it loses the ability to store value. Gold has long been the reigning champion of sound money, but it has very real limitations that are impossible to overcome.

---

# 6.
# EVERYONE NEEDS TO TRUST THE SYSTEM

"The root problem with conventional currency is all the trust that's required to make it work. The central bank must be trusted not to debase the currency, but the history of fiat currencies is full of breaches of that trust. Banks must be trusted to hold our money and transfer it electronically, but they lend it out in waves of credit bubbles with barely a fraction in reserve."

SATOSHI NAKAMOTO

---

WE RARELY THINK of paper as a technology, but when it was introduced to solve the physical challenges of gold and other precious metal coins, it revolutionized the financial world.

Paper money actually traces its roots back to ancient China, where it soon proved far more practical than carrying heavy coins. Over the centuries, this development spread worldwide, paving the way for an ever-evolving landscape of banknotes and financial innovations.

What started as a convenience, however, quickly evolved into something far more consequential. This chapter will demonstrate how the introduction of paper bills paved the way for a system that would thrive on abstraction and come to rely heavily on trust.

→»

Initially, paper money was straightforward: it was all fully backed by gold. People would deposit their gold coins in a bank and receive a receipt (called a *promissory note*)—a written promise stating how much gold the bank owed them. It was a simple system, with a 1:1 ratio of gold backing each note.

To claim their gold, a depositor would visit the bank with their promissory note—which would say something like, "*The Bank of St. Louis owes Natalie Brunell $10 worth of gold*," proving the identity of the original owner—and then physically receive their gold out of the vault.

Over time, banks recognized an opportunity for greater efficiency: transferable receipts. Rather than withdrawing your gold each time you needed to pay someone, you could simply hand them your paper receipt, allowing them to claim the gold at your bank instead. This innovation turned personal banknotes into bearer instruments— much like arcade tokens or gift cards—meaning that whoever held the note could redeem it for gold. As a result, people no longer had to lug around heavy coins and could conduct business more easily.

Transfer of ownership became far more efficient with paper bills, which were lighter and safer to carry than gold. Nothing else had changed—banks still maintained that 1:1 match between each bill and the gold in their vaults.

Behind the scenes, these paper instruments also simplified recordkeeping: instead of rummaging through the vault for every transaction, bankers could simply credit and debit accounts. If I needed to pay my neighbor $100, the banker would just deduct $100 from my "ledger" and add $100 to my neighbor's—without ever leaving their desk.

→»

As trade expanded and merchant networks grew, banks began honoring not only their own promissory notes, but also each others'—as long as they were confident in each bank's solvency. This interbank trust accelerated the adoption of paper currency.

Because it was so much easier, people increasingly left their gold in the banks for storage and protection, opting to simply trade notes representing the "real thing."

In the U.S., long before the introduction of the standardized dollar bills we use today, each bank actually issued its own unique banknotes. (A quick internet search of "old banknotes" reveals a fascinating variety of designs from banks you've likely never heard of, highlighting how decentralized and varied this system once was!)

We are now so accustomed to the abstraction of money—sending money instantaneously via Venmo and PayPal without any paper changing hands—that it's hard to imagine what a dramatic shift it really was to move to bank notes. (In point of fact, these transactions are only "instantaneous" as far as we're concerned—but more on that later.)

But relying on notes to represent gold meant placing trust in intermediaries—often referred to as *counterparties*—and accepting the inherent risk that they might fail to honor their promises. This is known as *counterparty risk*.

-»»

*Trust* is the operative word.

Remember the rulers who succumbed to the temptation of coin clipping? Something similar happened with the ratio of paper bills to gold stored in vaults. Paper was so convenient that people rarely came to claim their *actual* gold, and almost never did so all at once.

In medieval Italy, bankers discovered they could keep just a portion of each depositor's gold in their vaults while lending out more than they physically held. For example, with $100 in gold deposits, a bank might issue $1,000 in paper notes, counting on the fact that not all depositors would return to claim their gold at the same time. By earning interest on these extra loans, they ushered in a new approach to banking—one that would prove both profitable and transformational.

Does this ring a bell? This is the very same process of *fractional reserve banking* we discussed in Chapter Four.[37]

**Soon, *issuing more claims on the gold than there was gold* itself became standard banking practice**.

The implications would be profound. Thomas Jefferson put a fine point on it: "Paper is poverty, it is only the ghost of money, and not money itself."

-»»

This practice of fractional reserve banking effectively expanded the amount of "money" circulating in the economy, a phenomenon, you'll recall, known as *monetary inflation*.

While the total amount of gold in banks' vaults stayed the same, the extra paper notes they issued created the illusion of more wealth, fueling economic growth and enabling more borrowing and lending.

But this illusion came at a cost. By relying on trust that everyone wouldn't demand their gold simultaneously, banks introduced quite a bit of fragility into the system. When trust faltered—sparked by anything from a newspaper headline to a town rumor—it triggered financial panics. People would rush to redeem their paper notes for gold that didn't actually exist in sufficient quantities.

This system of issuing more claims to gold than banks had on hand planted the seeds of mistrust. The resulting erosion of confidence would periodically ripple through the entire financial system, setting the stage for the repeated economic shocks that led many to call for stabilizing an increasingly wild and unpredictable banking and monetary system.

↠

**Whether we realize it or not, our relationship with banks is based on a structurally precarious system of *trust*. We trust the banks to operate honestly, but they're playing an entirely different game.**

If you've ever bought a ticket on an overbooked flight, you'll have a sense of how things can easily go awry. When every ticketed passenger shows up, there aren't enough seats on the plane to uphold the number of "promises" the airline has made. If you're among the last to arrive, you may not be able to redeem the service you've already paid for.

This situation can be easily remedied if flexible passengers volunteer to take a different flight. For banks, however, there is no such workaround. When they issue more banknotes than they have cash to back them up, the last people who try to claim their money are out of luck. *It's as if that money no longer exists* (that is, unless there's a central bank to serve as a backstop—but more on that a bit later!). The money's gone, and so is their chance of getting it back.

Fortunately, such occasions remain pretty rare for most of us in relatively stable societies like the U.S.—with the exception of several high-profile bank failures in 2023 after the Covid-19 pandemic.

But that confidence in banks isn't uniformly shared throughout the rest of the world, where shifting conditions often mean that people can't always access their own savings. For example, investment strategist Lyn Alden opens her book *Broken Money* with the jaw-dropping story of a desperate young woman in Lebanon who, during a major financial crisis in 2022 in which banks had frozen customers' assets, resorted to pulling a fake gun to demand her *own* money from her *own* bank in order to pay for her sister's medical treatments.[38]

→»

Like kids left alone with a cookie jar, governments and banks have long demonstrated little resistance to the temptations of paper money. It has, over time, distorted the banking system—sometimes beyond recognition.

It's easy to see why banks, motivated by profit, increasingly embraced fractional reserve practices. In the U.S., while banks did maintain at least *some* connection to gold until the 20th century (except during multiple war periods), the writing was certainly on the wall for them to chip away at that ratio.

If they'd started out keeping 95% of their cash in reserves, say— lending out just 5% of their deposits for a little extra profit—why not whittle that down to 75%, or 50% … or eventually even lower than 3% (their absurdly over-leveraged position leading up to the 2008 Great Financial Crisis) and rake in the interest on the loans?[39] As a profit-seeking enterprise, wouldn't it be irresponsible *not to*?

The banks were willing to take the risks associated with decoupling from gold because the upside was so enormous.

→»

The early days of the "free banking" era in the U.S., in which thousands of different banks issued proprietary notes that were often worthless and unredeemable just a few miles away, were undeniably chaotic. The era has been painted as a bit of a Wild West of banking, and there's definitely some truth to that reputation.

But this approach also offered real-time corrections for poor management. Banks that took excessive risks with their clients' money (by, say, making bad loans to people who'd demonstrated little creditworthiness and ultimately couldn't pay back what they'd borrowed) would be naturally washed out of the system. This would be devastating to those who'd entrusted those banks with their money, to be sure, but the damage would be limited to a relatively small pool of people and would caution other banks to act with greater wisdom and restraint.

However, when local bank failures began to multiply, fear of contagion would spread throughout the financial system. Smaller banks, facing cash shortages and panicky withdrawals, would scramble to borrow from larger institutions like JPMorgan (whose banking empire eventually became today's JPMorgan Chase) to stay afloat. Because these banks were so heavily interconnected—serving as one another's counterparties—a single collapse could trigger a domino effect. As each bank turned to ever-larger institutions to cover their own shortfalls, pressure would ripple up the system and through to the world's most powerful banks.[40]

Even the biggest banks eventually grew uneasy, aware that unchecked failures below could very well threaten their own solvency.

⇢⇢

It's like the classic trope of a wealthy teenager: knowing their parents will always bail them out, they take risks they'd never dream of if they had to face the consequences alone. When someone else is willing to foot the bill, recklessness starts to feel like a reasonable choice.

Those big banks eventually grew tired of bailing out smaller ones. The tipping point arrived with an event known as the Panic of 1907, when a speculative gamble on copper led by two Montana brothers failed, toppling the New York bank that had financed them.[41] The resulting shockwaves spread across the banking system until a last-minute cash injection from J.P. Morgan and other wealthy financiers halted the crisis.[42]

This panic forced Americans to confront the flaws of a mostly decentralized banking system. Although the United States had attempted central banks before,[43] the efforts never took permanent root and had faced significant pushback. Now, however, many felt there was a need for more stability, oversight, and coordination. In the wake of 1907, both the bankers and the general public began pushing harder for reforms, paving the way for a more centralized financial framework that would bring standardization to an industry facing rapid growth and movement.

Seizing the moment, a small, powerful group—a mix of politicians and bankers with deep connections—stepped in to address those challenges and, in the process, consolidate their own power.

→»

Few of us are familiar with the story of how six men representing nearly a quarter of the world's wealth[44] came together in 1910, under cloak of night, to "write a plan to reform the nation's banking system."*

Each brought his own unique personality, interests, blind spots, and idiosyncrasies; together, they designed the Federal Reserve System (see Chapter Four), an institution that has arguably shaped modern history more than any other on Earth.

The *Federal Reserve Act*, passed by Congress in 1913, established a central banking system in the U.S. that would go on to impact the global economy—an influence that continues to this day, shaped by the decisions of a small group of individuals as human and fallible as any of us.

It's important to bear in mind that while the creators of that system may have been responding to a real need, they were not gathering as philanthropists: they knew all too well how the plan would protect and expand their own vast wealth.

-→»

The Fed was established not only to unify the banking system and issue Federal Reserve Bank notes (dollar bills) as a national currency, but also to absorb risk, boost confidence, and prevent the bank runs that always loomed like the threat of wildfire.

That's why many bankers and businesses supported the establishment of the Fed as a *lender of last resort* and a permanent safeguard: if a contagion of doubt began to spread through the system, the big banks no longer had to step in and help out with

---

* At the beginning, the Fed was limited in how much it could expand the money supply because each dollar in circulation had to be supported by 40 cents worth of gold in the vaults. In this way, the Fed's power was very much constrained: if it wanted to issue more currency, it needed either to secure more gold or loan more money to businesses producing tangible goods.

their own reserves. The Fed would be there to issue more money and prevent financial catastrophe.

→»

But the Fed's ability to intervene and absorb smaller shocks—shocks that would have caused bank closures in an earlier era—has allowed the system to grow unnaturally resilient.

Banks have become "too big to fail," meaning that they're so crucial to a functioning economy that the government must go to extraordinary lengths to protect them from the consequences of their own risk-taking. They're so powerful, in other words, that they (paradoxically) render the system infinitely more fragile.

Instead of limiting damage to one segment of the system, like a wound which could be bandaged and healed, centralization in the Fed meant that most crises have become systemic, the way diseases of the human circulatory or nervous systems affect the whole body.

In other words, failures no longer result in course correction; they're absorbed by the entire economy.

By printing money and rescuing failing institutions, government interventions shift the burden away from the banks and onto the public—massively redistributing wealth from the poor to the rich through inflation.

We've seen it time and again, from the Great Financial Crisis that destroyed my family's savings to the response to the Covid-19 pandemic that upended the global economy.

These major players—the institutions and their executives—walk away without a scratch, sometimes even securing huge bonuses, while the rest of us struggle to make ends meet.

Our system has become addicted to this process: money printing is the drug and the Fed is the supplier. What may have begun as potentially therapeutic has evolved into something deeply destructive; and, as with most addicts, the burdens are shared widely. In this case, the heaviest price is paid by society at large: the middle and working classes who watch their dollars lose value while reckless lending goes unchecked.

And yet, these institutions—the addicts' "dealers"—would soon be given the keys to the world's financial future.

–⟫

# Chapter 6 Summary

Gold's primary problem is its lack of portability, which made the transition to paper—for convenience—almost inevitable. But banks, realizing that people rarely came to claim their gold simultaneously, decided that they could issue more paper receipts than they had gold in their vaults, which drastically increased their profits but also introduced serious fragility into the system. Such practices led to recurring financial panics, and the resulting instability led to the formation of the Federal Reserve in 1913. The creation of the Fed interrupted natural market corrections and established the expansion of the money supply as a tempting solution to economic problems.

**Key Takeaway**: Paper money introduced a system based on trust and inflation.

# 7.
# EVERYONE
# WANTS
# DOLLARS

**"The dollar isn't just a currency—it's a
language the whole world speaks."**

JACK WELCH

———

THE U.S. DOLLAR—RECOGNIZED and trusted worldwide—is
now the undisputed king of currencies.

Whether we call them "bucks," "big ones," or "Benjamins," dollars
aren't just America's currency—they're the world's. Most Americans
can name only a few other currencies, but people almost everywhere
recognize the dollar as the global standard.

It's easy to assume this dominance comes simply from America's
power and influence. The U.S. has long been the biggest player in
the global economy, so naturally, the world would want its currency.

That's true, but it's only part of the story.

Less than a century ago, another small group of influential leaders anchored the dollar at the center of the global economy. In doing so, they redefined international trade, finance, and power itself.

Recognizing how this happened—and the Federal Reserve's role in shaping the transformation—is critical to understanding why the dollar became, and remains, the *global reserve currency*.

→»

The story begins with the unique position of the U.S. after World War II. But to really grasp that moment, we first need to look at the key events in the decades leading up to it.

As discussed in Chapter Six, the Federal Reserve was established in 1913, just before World War I, to act as a "bank for banks" and stabilize the financial system. At the time, the U.S. dollar was on the gold standard and legally convertible into a fixed amount of gold at $20.67 per ounce.

This meant that the Fed couldn't just print however much money it wanted. For every dollar it issued, the Fed needed 40 cents in gold reserves and the rest had to be backed by other safe assets, like commercial loans to solid businesses. To increase the money supply, the Fed had to acquire more gold or more of these commercial assets. While not a perfect 1:1 gold backing, this system kept the Fed's money-printing powers in check.

But global events soon tested these gold constraints, prompting policymakers to loosen them and pushing central banks worldwide into a far more influential role.

→»

Shortly after the establishment of the Fed, World War I erupted in Europe. War is devastating for humanity but often lucrative for business. While Europe descended into chaos, the U.S., neutral and an ocean away, was in a uniquely favorable position. The war fueled demand for American goods, spurring mass production and creating a windfall for the U.S. economy.

European nations suspended gold convertibility at home so they could print more of their own currencies to finance the war. At the same time, American banks extended large loans to European governments. In return, gold flowed into U.S. vaults, dramatically increasing both the Fed's reserves and America's economic influence. As the currencies of warring nations faltered, the U.S. dollar grew in prominence, boosting its international standing.[45]

—>>

When the U.S. entered World War I in 1917, the federal government needed massive amounts of money, and fast. The Fed's gold reserves had grown during the early war years thanks to booming exports and European borrowing, but gold standard rules still limited how much currency could be issued. Remember: by law, every dollar had to be backed by at least 40% gold, with the remaining 60% in "eligible paper," meaning those short-term commercial loans to businesses.

To raise funds, the Treasury sold war bonds to the public, appealing to their patriotism, while banks and other institutions also became major buyers. The problem was that when banks used a lot of their cash to buy bonds, they had less available for normal lending or to meet withdrawals.

If they needed more cash, they could go to the Federal Reserve and borrow, but under the 1913 strict rules, the Fed could only accept gold or commercial loans as collateral for issuing new currency, not government bonds.

In June 1917, Congress changed that. *The non-gold portion of the dollar's backing could now include U.S. government debt.* The Fed could accept bonds from banks as collateral for loans, count them toward the "eligible paper" reserve requirements, and issue more currency.[46] This made it easier to finance the war, but it also loosened the gold standard's discipline over the dollar.[47]

Such changes marked a permanent shift in the Federal Reserve's role. The collaboration between the government and the Fed during this period reshaped the relationship between money, debt, and gold, cementing the central bank's growing influence over U.S. economic policy.

*From a limited guardian of currency reserves, the Fed was effectively transformed into a central player in managing the U.S. financial system.*

The precedent was clear. When faced with urgent needs, monetary constraints could be abandoned. The money supply expanded and, not coincidentally, CPI shot up to nearly 18% in 1917 and stayed above 15% until 1921. This means that the dollar lost more than 40% of its purchasing power during that time.[48]

⇥

By the end of World War I, the United States had emerged as the world's largest creditor nation. Gold continued flowing in from European debt repayments, and the U.S. issued new loans to help rebuild shattered economies. To support the recovery, the Federal Reserve also lowered interest rates. This made borrowing cheaper and encouraged American investment capital to flow overseas, partly to relieve pressure on weak European currencies.

But easy credit abroad also meant easy credit at home. Cheap money, loosened financial regulations, and post-war optimism fueled the "Roaring Twenties," a period of heavy speculation and rising debt. Many people used that cheap credit to invest in the stock market or finance lavish lifestyles, creating an illusion of endless prosperity.

Beneath the surface, though, debt levels far exceeded the actual money supply, creating a massive credit bubble. When it burst in 1929, the global financial system collapsed, triggering the Great Depression. It was a decade marked by bank failures, mass unemployment, and widespread poverty.

→»

By the 1930s, much of the world was in deep economic turmoil. Europe, still burdened by World War I debts, struggled to rebuild. Governments tried to keep up the appearance of maintaining the gold standard but quietly printed money to survive: Britain doubled its money supply, France tripled theirs, and Germany quadrupled its own to meet crushing reparation payments under the Treaty of Versailles.[49]

In Germany, this reckless money printing led to *hyperinflation*— wiping out savings, destabilizing the government, and plunging millions into poverty. Economic chaos fueled political extremism. Adolf Hitler exploited public despair and humiliation to rally support for his authoritarian ambitions. Economic volatility, institutional breakdown, and rising nationalism created a dangerous powder keg.

Meanwhile, in the U.S., the general infrastructure remained physically untouched by war and the nation still held 40% of the world's gold reserves, a very large share.[50] But the Great Depression had pushed unemployment above 20% by 1933. Thousands of banks failed in just three years, shaking confidence in the financial system and prompting large-scale withdrawals. The turmoil convinced authorities that more dramatic action was needed to restore stability.[51]

At the height of this crisis, the U.S. suspended domestic gold convertibility, and, through Executive Order, required citizens to surrender their gold to the government. Private gold ownership was largely banned, marking a dramatic assertion of federal control over money.[52]

In 1934, the government raised the official gold price from $20.67 to $35 an ounce, effectively devaluing the dollar. This meant that the same amount of gold in U.S. vaults was now worth nearly 70% more in dollar terms. The increase expanded the paper value of the nation's reserves, which in turn allowed the Fed to issue more currency. By loosening this constraint, the government aimed to fight the steep fall in prices that had followed the 1929 crash.

The devaluation, along with new banking laws passed by Congress, helped restore some public confidence and slowed the wave of bank runs. Gold flowed into the United States as foreign holders took advantage of the higher price and sought the relative safety of the American economy. But the move also set another precedent: when economic pressures mounted, the strict limits of the gold standard could be set aside.

It would take decades for the full consequences of this decision to play out.

—»

By the eve of World War II, the U.S. held the most valuable gold reserves in history and a ready industrial base unmatched anywhere in the world, leaving it uniquely positioned to finance and equip the Allies.

When the war broke out in 1939, American factories roared to life, producing goods and supplies at a staggering scale. Millions went to work, and unemployment fell to historic lows.

The U.S. was now the world's military and economic arsenal.

World War II lasted six years, tragically claiming between 45 and 50 million lives and devastating much of Europe and East Asia.[53] As it drew to a close, it was obvious that global recovery would require immense sums of money.

-»>

In July 1944, as the war drew to an end, delegates from 44 nations met at the picturesque Mount Washington Hotel in Bretton Woods, New Hampshire, to design a new international monetary order.[54]

This new system would be centered around a *new* global reserve currency (the asset central banks hold for safety and settlement).*

**The outcome of that conference, known as the Bretton Woods Agreement, officially crowned the U.S. dollar as that global reserve currency, putting America definitively at the center of global finance**.

Since "Bretton Woods," as it came to be known, central banks have primarily held U.S. dollars in the form of Treasuries. At the time, those dollars were redeemable for gold at $35 an ounce, but as we'll see, that convertibility ultimately would not last. In effect, the dollar replaced gold as the world's preferred store of value for official reserves and cross-border payments, underpinning global financial stability.

Bretton Woods was the recovery plan for a global society ravaged by decades of economic unrest and war. The old system had taken centuries to evolve; three weeks was long enough, it turns out, to craft a new one. Gold would still play a (diminished) role in this new world order, but its days as the primary reserve asset were numbered.

-»>

---

* Historians generally trace the succession of dominant global reserve currencies from the Spanish silver dollar (1500s–1600s) to the Dutch guilder (1600s–late 1700s), the British pound sterling (early 1800s–early 1900s), and the U.S. dollar (mid-1900s–present).

# Chapter 7 Summary

In the first half of the 20th century, the U.S. rose from a promising economic power to the architect of a new global financial order. The massive costs of two world wars prompted policymakers to loosen gold's backing of the dollar.

At the 1944 Bretton Woods Conference, the dollar was officially crowned the world's reserve currency, with a predetermined amount of gold initially required as backing. This arrangement effectively placed the dollar at the center of global trade and finance.

**Key Takeaway**: By marrying the credibility of gold with America's industrial and economic dominance, Bretton Woods cemented the dollar as the cornerstone of the post-war global economy.

# 8.
# EVERYONE FEELS THE IMPACT

"The curious task of economics is to demonstrate
to men how little they really know about
what they imagine they can design."

FRIEDRICH HAYEK

———————————

I T'S EASY TO see why, in the 1940s, the U.S. dollar was crowned the global reserve currency. Like a prom queen basking in universal admiration, the dollar had everything going for it: a country awash in vast natural resources, and the unmatched advantage of being spared the devastation of war. The dollar seemed stable, well-governed, and shielded from the authoritarian impulses that plagued other nations.

The Bretton Woods Agreement ensured that U.S. dollars would be held by other countries mainly in the form of Treasury bills (short-term government-issued IOUs promising repayment with interest after a fixed term). These bills were considered "as good as gold."[55]

Think of Bretton Woods as a global handshake on fixed exchange rates: every major currency linked its value to the dollar, and the dollar promised redemption in gold at $35 an ounce. This arrangement made the dollar the centerpiece of global trade and finance, creating a system where much of the world's gold reserves flowed into U.S. vaults.

**Figure 7: Global reserve currency**

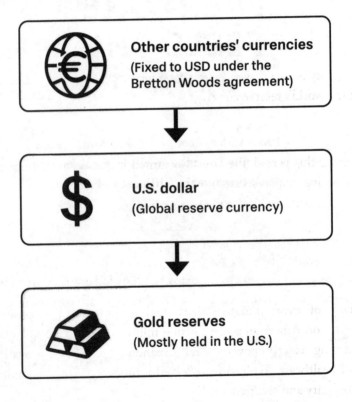

But there was a catch: everyone had to *trust* (there's that word again!) the U.S. government not to print too much money beyond the amount of gold in its vaults.

Spoiler alert: it did.

↦

With World War II in the rearview mirror, America radiated with a sense of expectation, expansion, and promise. The United States found itself in a position of immense power and privilege. Relieved of the constraints of wartime rationing and eager to embrace a brighter future, consumer demand exploded: from cars and homes to appliances and furniture, Americans went shopping.[56]

By all logic, the Fed could have taken its foot off the gas once the war ended—but it didn't. Policymakers, fearing a deep post-war slump that never materialized, continued suppressing interest rates by intervening in the government bond market, even as the economy boomed and America assumed its new role as the issuer of the world's reserve currency.

↦

During this period, the U.S. also turned its focus to creating and expanding major social programs. These included the G.I. Bill in the 1940s, which provided returning servicemen with housing and education benefits; the Social Security Act amendments of 1950, which expanded income support for retirees; and later, in 1965, Medicare and Medicaid, which provided health coverage for seniors and low-income individuals, respectively.

Many of these initiatives have had a profound and positive impact on American society, lifting millions into the middle class, reducing elderly poverty, and expanding access to education and healthcare. Their aims reflected a broader vision of national prosperity and security.

However, payroll taxes and regular tax revenues covered only part of the tab. To make up the difference, the U.S. increasingly engaged in expansive monetary policy without a corresponding rise in gold reserves. While these programs delivered meaningful benefits, they also introduced hidden costs, gradually loosening the nation's monetary discipline and laying early groundwork for future financial imbalances.

At the same time, America was financing costly and deadly military engagements abroad, including the Korean War in the 1950s and the Vietnam War in the 1960s—adding further strain to the nation's finances.

As the issuer of the world's new reserve currency, the U.S. entered a phase sometimes called a "deficit without tears": America could run large trade and budget deficits without immediately feeling the inflationary consequences at home.

But there's a reason we have the saying "there's no such thing as a free lunch."

⇥

It's worth quickly pointing out the difference between "debt" and "deficits," since sometimes these words are used interchangeably. A deficit is the shortfall in a single year's budget—what the government spends beyond what it collects—while the debt is the running total of all those yearly deficits added together.

In practice, it's like the U.S. has a credit card with no spending limit—and, again, when the bill comes due, it just pays it off with another credit card.

Can you imagine getting away with that?

If you and I didn't *work* (an important word—we'll come back to it!) to pay down our loans every month, but instead could keep rolling the bills onto never-ending credit cards, we'd be able to delay things for a while, too. But pretty soon we'd be drowning in debt and the collectors would come to recoup whatever they could from us. Maybe our cars would be repossessed, or maybe we'd be evicted from our homes. One way or another, the bill would actually need to be paid with real money and not just future promises.

Government debts, on the other hand, are never truly repaid: they just accrue over time as new debt is issued to pay off old debt. When you hear about ballooning federal debt, this is what it means.

For this reason, other countries that had accumulated large reserves of U.S. dollars started to worry that the U.S. might not have enough gold to back all the dollars in circulation. Confidence in the dollar's ability to maintain its gold value started to erode.

The Bretton Woods system, built on trust in the dollar and its gold backing, began to falter, as foreign nations grew increasingly skeptical of the dollar's stability.

—»

By the 1960s, this unease turned into action as some countries began repatriating their gold—exchanging their dollars for the gold held in U.S. vaults. This created a serious problem for the system: while the dollar was supposed to be "as good as gold," there was far less gold in U.S. reserves than dollars circulating worldwide.

The situation was akin to that overbooked flight mentioned in Chapter Six, but on a much larger scale. Instead of hoping that a few passengers wouldn't show up to claim their seats, the entire monetary system was now based on the hope that the vast majority of claimants wouldn't come to claim their gold at once, only to discover that their tickets—in this case, their dollars—were merely empty promises.

To put it more bluntly: a number of nations felt the U.S. could no longer be trusted to maintain the gold standard, and feared that their dollars would continue losing value.

—»

The drain on U.S. gold reserves that took place during this period put significant pressure on the system, just as U.S. debts and obligations were increasing.

The U.S. had abused its privilege as the operator of the world's money printer, and other nations were outraged that monetary inflation caused by American policies was jeopardizing the security of their gold in U.S. vaults. These countries had handed over their gold in exchange for dollars, trusting the dollar's promise of stability and convertibility. But because the U.S. had flooded the system with too much printed money, confidence in the dollar began to crumble, and they wanted their gold back.

As more nations exchanged their dollars for gold, U.S. reserves dwindled to a dangerously low level. The fragile balance underpinning the Bretton Woods system—where every dollar was meant to be backed by a certain quantity of gold—was increasingly untenable.

By the 1960s, the world's gold supply that had concentrated in U.S. vaults after World War II had begun flowing back out. Since the dollar was its bedrock, this threatened to bring down the entire global monetary system.

↠

The situation came to a head in 1971. In a televised speech on August 15 of that momentous year, President Richard Nixon surprised the world with an announcement that came to be known as the "Nixon Shock": *dollars would no longer be redeemable for gold.*

It was as though a bank teller, with a line of customers snaking out the door, suddenly pulled down the rolling shutter and abruptly stated, without explanation, "We're closed." In one fell swoop, the Bretton Woods system was finished.

**This "suspension" of redeemability of dollars for gold was never reversed. In that moment, the true *fiat* system—a dollar backed by nothing but IOUs—was born.**

→»

You may be asking yourself: how did the U.S. remain the global reserve currency after defaulting on its gold convertibility and causing worldwide economic instability?

Much of the answer lies in strategic diplomacy and the creation of a system that many refer to as the *petrodollar*. After the shock of the 1971 decision to end the dollar's link to gold, the U.S. needed a way to ensure global demand for its currency. In the 1970s, it struck a deal with oil-producing nations, particularly Saudi Arabia, to *trade oil—the world's most critical commodity—exclusively in U.S. dollars.*

The establishment of the petrodollar system in the 1970s (an arrangement that officially ended in 2024, after 50 years), orchestrated by Henry Kissinger and other key government figures, was crucial in securing and extending the U.S. dollar's hegemony.

This arrangement dictated that countries buying oil had to hold large reserves of dollars.

Oil producers would invest their earnings in U.S. Treasury bonds, creating a cycle that propped up the dollar's value and extended America's global economic power.

By ensuring constant global demand for the dollar, the U.S. was able to once again finance growing deficits.

At least for a while.

→»

In the pages that follow, we'll unpack exactly how this "reserve currency bonus" turned into a double-edged sword. While it gave the U.S. enormous global power and helped fund the expansion of government social programs that millions rely on, the very same bonus has also contributed—perhaps unintentionally—to the decline of the American working class and has quietly stolen from future generations.

The pain that many Americans are feeling today—the hollowing out of the middle class and skyrocketing cost of housing and healthcare, for example—are, in fact, *directly connected to the U.S.'s status as the global reserve currency.*

⇻

Let's take a closer look.

Not too long ago, the U.S. was a powerhouse of industry: from consumer goods to innovative technology, Americans produced more than they consumed. The U.S. made things! American entrepreneurship and community spirit—not to mention the infrastructure, like schools and highways, that supported it all— earned its reputation, all over the world, as the land of opportunity and the beacon of hope that called out to families like mine.

That hope was symbolically represented by a number of truly "American" products. I recall my mom telling me stories of her young life in Poland, when everyone wanted things that were made in the U.S.A. Among the most prized items, she told me, were iconic American blue jeans. As Levi Strauss & Co. put it, those jeans "represented freedom and independence"[57] to people everywhere, particularly in Eastern Europe.

To the dismay of many both at home and abroad, that glittering image has faded in recent years. Even Levi's jeans *themselves* are produced almost entirely outside the U.S. Nowadays, if you look at the tags on your clothes or the stickers on many of your household products, you'll notice (if you haven't already!) that they are often made in Asia.

If a product is "Made in the USA," that fact is often broadcast quite loudly on the packaging. It signifies that the manufacturer has in some way overcome the barriers now associated with manufacturing stateside, or tacitly acknowledges that its target customer base will opt to pay a little bit more for products made at home.

→»

*What's behind this?*

While trade policy certainly plays a role, there's a phenomenon called the Triffin Dilemma that reveals the inherent conflict between national economic interests and global obligations when a country's currency serves as the world's reserve.

Because the dollar plays this role, foreign central banks must hold substantial sums of it to settle trade and steady their own finances. The surest way to acquire those dollars is to sell goods—electronics, oil, clothing—into the U.S. market and accept payment in dollars. Thus, goods stream into America while dollars stream out, sustaining a built-in, global demand for U.S. currency.

Those constant trade deficits are the built-in price of having the dollar remain the world's reserve currency.

While this system ensures the global economy has access to dollars, it comes, as we've noted, at a cost: American industries have faced increased competition from cheaper foreign goods and services. As manufacturing shifts overseas to capitalize on lower costs, domestic jobs disappear and wages stagnate. The working class bears the brunt of these changes. Over time, as fewer well-paying jobs remain in the United States, this erosion of the industrial base deepens economic inequality and weakens the middle class.

Running a trade deficit for a few years isn't necessarily problematic, but when it lasts for decades, it becomes structural and difficult to reverse. The trade deficit might seem like an advantageous exchange of U.S. paper IOUs for products, but in reality, we're trading away valuable assets—like company shares and land—instead. Rather than building long-term wealth, we're funding short-term consumption. Over time, foreign investors end up owning more of U.S. businesses and government debt, leaving us with fewer assets for the future.

By the last quarter of the 20th century, the U.S. was importing far more than it was producing and exporting. Behind the outward dominance of the dollar was an economy that had become increasingly hollow. In essence, by consuming more than it was producing, the U.S. was slowly abandoning the foundation that had once propelled it to global superpower status.

In other words, **the privileges of being the global reserve currency often mask a deeper story, where the costs and benefits don't fall equally on all Americans**.

⇻

When factories closed and production slipped overseas, America didn't fall apart—it reinvented itself around money rather than manufacturing. Profits shifted from building cars or washing machines to building portfolios: bundling mortgages, trading stocks by the millisecond, and slicing debts into ever-thinner "investments." That transformation—called *financialization*—let Wall Street, big banks, and real-estate moguls mint fortunes even as assembly-line jobs disappeared.

At the same time, money poured into the rising tech sector, fueling a new kind of wealth centered around software, platforms, and speculation on the digital frontier. Simply put, the economy's power center moved from shop floors to trading floors, so those who manage money now reap the gains that once went to people who made tangible things.

Historically, finance existed primarily to provide capital to support productive economic activity—banks would lend money to businesses to build factories, buy equipment, and hire workers. *In a financialized economy, however, finance becomes an end in itself.*

Profit is generated more from speculation, trading financial products, and leveraging debt than from producing or selling actual goods and services.

If the idea of consumer products makes intuitive sense to you but the concept of mortgage-backed securities (one of the key drivers of the 2008 financial crisis) feels alien and deliberately confusing, you're not alone and you're not wrong to raise an eyebrow.

⟶⟩

Though Wall Street calls them "products," these financial instruments bear only the slightest resemblance to the word as we all understand it. With fewer goods to sell in the international marketplace, the U.S. has leveraged its status as the world's reserve currency in ways that are often very risky.

Whereas in the "free banking" era, failures due to excessive risk-taking might result in bank closures, these "too big to fail" banks have no incentive to take precautions. Banks and financial institutions know that the Fed always has their back: in 2008, the government bailed them out to the tune of approximately $498 billion, or 3.5 % of GDP.[58]

Hard-working Americans are always there to absorb the costs.

⟶⟩

Put another way, this new economy pretty much excludes the very workers whose industriousness helped make it possible for the U.S.

to become the reserve currency in the first place, and places the burden on all Americans to make up the difference. And if a central bank can debase the currency, then it can funnel resources towards the government's own priorities, largely out of view from the public.

Central bankers and politicians are able to devise novel methods for steering the economy in the direction they feel it should go, limited only by the beliefs, imaginations, and worldviews of the specific people in charge at any given moment. When the money supply can be controlled and managed by those in power, that power is inevitably centralized and further consolidated in fewer and fewer hands.

**This isn't a criticism of any individual, group, or political party. Rather, it's a structural flaw that underscores the wisdom of the American vision: a system deliberately designed to prevent unchecked centralization.**

Without consistent checks and balances and a structure of distributed power, the safeguards meant to protect against authoritarianism erode, allowing the very concentration of authority America's Founding Fathers designed the system to prevent.

It's important to recognize that the global shift away from hard money was likely neither purely accidental nor purely the result of a group of scheming, all-knowing masterminds. As we saw in Chapter Six, it was perhaps an almost inevitable consequence of gold's physical limitations as a global currency—its lack of portability, inefficiency in large-scale transactions, and vulnerability to centralization. These defects made centralization not just convenient, but necessary within the framework of an increasingly interconnected global economy.

**The fact of the matter is, the conditions were all there for a system of rules to give way to a system of rulers. And in a world where**

**the flow of money can be tightened or loosened, it's the hand on the spigot that ends up controlling everything else**.

⇢

To be clear, this isn't an argument against the U.S. dollar remaining the global reserve currency. The dollar's role *has* provided stability and facilitated trade on an unprecedented scale. But the unintended consequences of this system—endless debt creation, extreme wealth concentration, and financial instability—make it clear: we need a more measured, resilient approach for the future.

While the dollar could still be used as the world's currency for trade, we might instead envision a *neutral* reserve asset—one that can be held as a lasting store of value that isn't subject to manipulation through the policies, priorities, or whims of any single government or central authority.

In the chapters ahead, we'll explore how Bitcoin, with its fixed supply, decentralized design, and transparency, has the properties of a compelling *global reserve asset* to help support national currencies and return us to a hard money standard.

⇢

As a reminder, when a currency is simply issued by a government—without being backed by anything else—it's known as *fiat*. Rather than being pegged to a real-world commodity that has widely recognized value, the currency is simply backed by government promises (such as "the full faith and credit of the U.S. government") and the military strength behind them.

In a world operating on the gold standard, nature is the anchor (or peg) and paper money is simply an abstract representation of the real item of value. Without a limited natural resource to anchor its value, money on a *fiat standard* is entirely dependent upon the imperfect human beings controlling its flow from the central bank.

-»»

The gradual decline of the gold standard was a decades-long process of decoupling, culminating in the dollar's complete break from gold in 1971.

Since then, the global economy has entered truly uncharted territory.

-»»

## Chapter 8 Summary

Increased government spending post World War II led to more dollars circulating than there was gold to back them. Foreign governments began once again exchanging their dollars for gold, depleting U.S. gold reserves. In 1971, President Nixon abruptly ended the dollar's convertibility into gold, fundamentally transforming the global economic landscape. Instead of basing money on gold's natural scarcity, the dollar became dependent on the judgment of central bankers and politicians. This was the beginning of the *fiat* era—money backed only by government promises.

**Key Takeaway**: When the dollar was untethered from gold, the world lost its last anchor of monetary scarcity. This shift reshaped the entire domestic and global economic landscape.

# 9.
# EVERYONE
# PAID THE
# PRICE

**"Few things are as permanent as
temporary measures."**

**ALEX GLADSTEIN**

---

T HE LONG-TERM EFFECTS of the U.S. decision to go off the
gold standard in 1971 could not have been more dramatic or
consequential.

By nearly every metric, a major fork in the road had appeared,
vividly illustrated by the chart below showing the widening gap
between worker compensation and productivity. There was the
world before the "Nixon Shock," and a very different one afterward.

Chart 3 tracks two lines: productivity—how much a worker turns
out in an hour—and average pay. The lines moved closely together
until the early 1970s. But when the dollar decoupled from gold,
productivity kept climbing while wages barely budged, meaning

the extra output boosted company profits and investor returns, not workers' paychecks.

**Chart 3: Productivity growth and hourly compensation growth (1948–2024)**

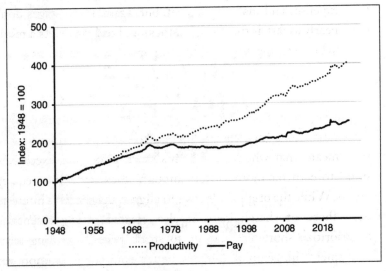

Source: Economic Policy Institute, U.S. Bureau of Labor Statistics.

*But why?*

Remember, whenever new money is pumped into the economy, it flows first to those closest to the source: large corporations, the wealthy, and the well-connected. These "big fish" typically channel it into ventures or financial instruments that can generate more profit over time. Companies, by and large, focus on maximizing returns on their capital—not on boosting wages for the people who work for them.

Raising wages is typically viewed as an ongoing cost rather than an investment that appreciates over time. For those closest to the money supply, funneling money into assets is tangibly and directly profitable. If, on the other hand, money held its value, investing in workers and growing their business would be far more attractive.

Meanwhile, as we've discussed, most wage earners don't own assets like stocks or real estate, at least not nearly to the same degree as their wealthy counterparts. They depend on their paychecks to cover their expenses and make ends meet, but, again, those wages don't grow nearly as fast as the prices of stocks and real estate. As a result, the gap between the wealthy and everyone else continues to widen.

→»

Beginning in the 1980s, executive compensation in many large corporations became increasingly tied to stock performance. This shift meant that when a company's stock price rose, executives stood to earn far more—often through stock options or equity grants. While the original idea was to align management's interests with those of shareholders, it also created strong incentives to prioritize short-term boosts to stock prices over long-term investments like employee wages, better equipment, or improved working conditions.

The result? Since the 1970s, average CEO compensation has soared more than 1,000%—from about 20 times the pay of a typical worker to nearly 300 times today.[59]

A common tactic companies often use is the *stock buyback*. A buyback is exactly what it sounds like: a company uses its extra cash to purchase its own shares, reducing the number available on the market. With fewer shares outstanding, each remaining share becomes more valuable, helping lift the stock price. Stock buybacks aren't inherently problematic, but starting in the 1980s, after regulations were loosened and cheap money increasingly flooded the system, companies spent enormous sums on buybacks—often using low-interest debt to fund them.

For example, in 2022, S&P 500 companies spent more than $900 billion on stock buybacks—an all-time high.[60] Like most other incentives to maximize return on investment, the stock buyback benefits shareholders and executives, whose pay is largely tied to stock performance, at the expense of investments in employees or production.

The result is a deepening imbalance in our economy, where the benefits of ownership continue to compound while the ordinary worker treads water.

→→

The working class has been squeezed from all directions.

Take the iconic can of Campbell's Tomato Soup, the price of which remained relatively consistent for over 75 years before launching into a nearly unstoppable upward trajectory since—you guessed it!—the early-to-mid 1970s.

And even a cursory glance at the next graph, showing cumulative inflation over the course of a century, tells a similarly compelling story that might be a bit familiar by now: *something dramatic occurred at that time*, and its impact has never abated.

## Chart 4: Cumulative price index inflation for all U.S. urban consumers (1950–2025)

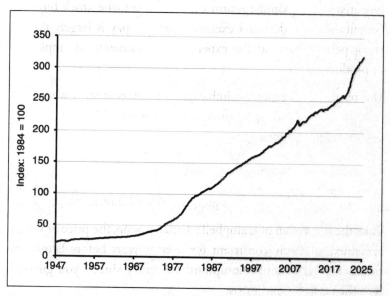

Source: Federal Reserve Bank of Minneapolis, U.S. Bureau of Labor Statistics.

By nearly every metric and on nearly every graph charting the course of the U.S. economy over time, *there's a striking shift in and around the pivotal year of 1971.*

The dollar's final break from gold was like the removal of a dam; the waters came gushing, fast and furious, unleashing forces that couldn't possibly be contained or reversed by the system that had released them.

⇶

The moment gold exited the equation and money was transformed from the weight of gold into a government promise, its value was left to rise or fall according to political decisions alone. We had entered the era of *fiat.*

Fiat isn't issued according to a particular schedule or with respect to any constraining factor, like redeemability for gold. Instead, it's driven by the expansion or contraction of credit, a decision made, as you now know, by the authorities with their hands on the financial spigot.

As the U.S. fell further and further behind in terms of global manufacturing, its economy didn't just give up and collapse; it pivoted, as we discussed in Chapter Eight, from *production* to *financialization*.

In an economy anchored by hard money, that amount of credit could not be expanded on a whim or printed from nothing. But when banks don't have to stick to that rule, they're free to make all sorts of aggressive bets. It's even easier when they know there's a *lender of last resort*—the Fed—that'll swoop in and rescue them if it turns out that they've made a miscalculation.

On second thought, calling it a miscalculation is inaccurate. When banks make risky bets, they aren't misjudging the odds—they're rationally responding to *a system that rewards risk-taking and socializes the losses*. This dynamic is known as *moral hazard*: when a party is protected from the consequences of failure, it has every incentive to take bigger risks.

From the banks' point of view, then, it would be irresponsible *not* to gamble—especially when they know the Federal Reserve stands ready to cover their losses if things go wrong.

--»

Once money is decoupled from something that can be objectively measured, the temptation to use the money printer to solve a government's most pressing problems proves irresistible.

Again, this isn't an indictment of any individual person, decision, or political party; it's a matter of pure incentives. For leaders of all stripes, public demand to make progress *now*—even if it means kicking the inevitable consequences down the road—is almost hard-wired.

It's no wonder, then, that politicians' promises (regardless of party) seem to lose value over time, much like the money they represent. Once individual banks were consolidated under the Federal Reserve and the printing press took over, the entire system became dependent on monetary expansion, the way an addict depends on a fix just to function.

This metaphor is particularly apt when we consider the law of diminishing returns associated with drugs: as a person slips further into addiction, they require more and more of the same substance to achieve any results at all.

→»

The fiat system has greatly benefited banks, corporations, and wealthy investors. Banks lend money, and, as inflation causes prices to go up, the value of hard assets like homes rises as well. When these assets are sold, owners make a profit, pay off their loans, and buy new assets, while the bank lends more money to the next buyer, collecting interest each time. This cycle continues, enriching both the sellers and the banks. Rinse, repeat.

As we've seen, in a system built on credit and driven by inflation, owning assets is the key to staying ahead. More money is created, prices rise, and assets like homes, stocks, and land climb in value. Cash loses purchasing power over time, making it a counterproductive savings vehicle.

**Inflation punishes savers. In a world anchored by hard money, saving would be the cornerstone of long-term planning and stability. It would fortify the future rather than erode it**.

And as we've already seen, assets like houses aren't becoming *more valuable* in any fundamental sense. Instead, as the supply of money expands, each dollar loses purchasing power—meaning it takes more dollars to buy the same things, just as we saw in our Monopoly example.

Wealthy individuals and corporations, those who already own assets, can spend freshly printed, cheaper dollars to buy even more of those assets *before* prices rise. By the time this new money makes its way through the economy, prices of everyday goods have gone up for everyone.

⇶

Much of today's monetary inflation doesn't represent real growth at all; it's actually debt masquerading as progress. The massive expansion of the money supply isn't magic, it's just borrowed into existence, creating an economy that looks like it's thriving when it's really just stacking up IOUs.

Imagine a business that isn't increasing production or expanding its client base, but keeps borrowing money to create an illusion of "growth." On the surface, everything looks great: revenues appear to rise, operations expand, and the headlines paint a picture of success. But underneath, lies nothing but mounting debt that will one day come due.

That's exactly what's happening globally. By 2023, the world's economy had grown to about $105 trillion,[61] but global debt has skyrocketed to a record $313 trillion.[62] This means that for every $1 of growth, we've taken on almost $2.50 of debt. If the U.S. Treasury was a private business, no bank would approve the loan! Yet we keep doubling down on the same strategy, needing ever-expanding debt to produce smaller and smaller returns.[63]

As of 2024 and for the first time in its history, the U.S. spends more of its budget paying the interest on its debt than it does on defense.[64] Its debt-fueled growth clearly isn't sustainable. As the debt piles up, the cost of *servicing* it—paying that interest—becomes a heavy drag on future growth. Just like an over-leveraged business, an economy can only borrow from the future for so long before the weight becomes unbearable.

So when you see the money supply expanding year after year, it's not a sign of health. It's a warning light.

Some economists may argue that government debt isn't like household debt and never really needs to be repaid, only rolled over. But this overlooks the limits of confidence, resources, and reality. You can't expand debt into the outer reaches of the galaxy forever.

Sooner or later and one way or another, the bill comes due—whether through inflation, taxation, default, or social breakdown. Our economy is desperately holding itself together with ever-increasing debt, and that debt will eventually have to be repaid.

→»

The flip side of that coin (pun somewhat intended) is a *deflationary* system, where prices keep falling and the purchasing power of money grows stronger over time. In this scenario, it's the savers, not the borrowers, who come out ahead, because their dollars will buy *more* goods and services in the future.

It's hard for us to envision such a world, but as Jeff Booth, author of *The Price of Tomorrow* points out, we only believe that inflation is natural and necessary because we've been living inside of a system that depends on that inflation to survive.[65]

→»

Falling prices feel, intuitively, like a good thing. It's wonderful, of course, when things that were once prohibitively expensive become affordable, like the personal computer or GPS systems—both of which originally cost thousands of dollars.[66] But deflation[67] is widely considered by governments and economists to be disastrous for an economy, because—in our current model—it suggests that the demand for goods has dropped (for any number of reasons) and that prices have to be lowered to compensate.

Booth argues, however, that there's an even deeper reason that deflation is feared within our current economic model: the model is built on *credit*, and deflation and credit make a toxic cocktail.

As we saw above, in a credit-based system, banks profit from loans over time: the longer it takes us to pay back a loan, the more interest the lender can earn. If prices fall, though, then the lender is in trouble; assets would be worth less at the end of the loan's term than they were when the money was originally borrowed.

Meanwhile, each dollar you owe becomes more valuable, making debt more expensive to repay. This can put added strain on borrowers, since the money used to pay off loans has greater purchasing power than when the debt was first incurred. As repayment becomes harder, defaults can rise and banks may scale back lending. If enough of this happens, credit dries up and the whole economy can grind to a halt.

Within a debt-soaked system like ours, that slowdown in lending is seen as a problem. But in an economy less dependent on debt, falling prices could actually be a feature, not a flaw. Goods would become more affordable and paychecks would stretch further. Savings would grow more powerful over time.

In such an environment, the benefits of economic growth would accrue more directly to workers and savers, rather than being siphoned off through interest payments to lenders.

→»

Perhaps now it's becoming clear that the Fed has a mandate to prop up the inflationary economy it has helped to create. In doing so, it has directly accelerated the frequency and severity of the very financial bubbles and crises it is also supposed to prevent.

When the global economy was rocked by the 2008 Great Financial Crisis (GFC), leaders faced a tough choice: let the overextended banks collapse and crash the global economy, or print enough money to bail 'em out because they were—again—simply *too big to fail.*

Over the prior decades, while many of us were busy living our lives, the financial system lost its connection with reality and became manic. Banks had made loans to people who couldn't possibly pay them, assuming that by the time the bill came due, the loan itself would be sold off as part of some vague financial "product" and become someone else's problem.

In a way, they were right: rather than suffering the consequences of their irresponsibility, most banks and bankers emerged from the crisis unscathed, with a new injection of freshly printed cash to reward them for their irresponsibility.

Instead, millions of ordinary people, like my parents, lost their homes. Unemployment skyrocketed. Looking to place blame, citizens retreated to their ideological corners and political polarization metastasized. The table was set for over a decade of inflation, shifting the burden to the next generation not only in the U.S., of course, but all around the world.

→»

We are all living under the shadow of the decisions surrounding the GFC and the inflation, palpable everywhere, that they wrought. Under such conditions, it has become impossible to save and impossible to get ahead: in fact, as we've discussed, inflation *disincentivizes* saving, because money banked for the future will be worth less than it is today.

From the teenager mowing lawns to buy their first car, to the young couple working towards a downpayment on a home, the effects of an unstable money system may be invisible, but they're keenly felt. Every year, our money loses value, and the chance of using today's earnings to secure future dreams slips further out of reach.

⇶

The 20th and early 21st centuries tell the story of a financial system cut loose from its real-world anchor—a system that has led us to where we are today. For everyday people, the situation feels like a trap: we can't save for the future unless we can find a way to secure and grow our purchasing power, but the tools to do so are built into a system that rewards access, not effort.

*Could there really be a way out of this mess?*

In an unknown location, a pseudonymous cryptographer, known only as "Satoshi Nakamoto," was quietly crafting an antidote.

⇶

# Chapter 9 Summary

Abandoning the gold standard forced the economic system to pivot to growth based on debt. Despite increased productivity, worker wages stagnated. Meanwhile, corporations took advantage of debt to maximize profits at all costs, particularly at the expense of employee compensation. Inequality deepened. Today, it's staggering to realize that it takes $3 of debt to produce $1 of economic growth! This is an unsustainable cycle in which monetary inflation masquerades as progress while wealth is silently transferred from working people to asset holders. Inflation, a "hidden tax" on ordinary workers, is required to keep the system afloat. Savers are punished, and borrowers and asset managers are rewarded.

**Key Takeaway**: Fiat systems rely on perpetual inflation to function—real growth is overshadowed by ballooning debt, and we largely have a situation where that debt is disguised as progress while money cannot serve as a reliable store of value.

# 10.
# EVERYONE'S ASKING: "WHAT IS BITCOIN?"

*"Writing a description for this thing for general audiences is bloody hard. There's nothing to relate it to."*

SATOSHI NAKAMOTO

---

THE BIRTH OF Bitcoin carries an almost mythological aura, often described as an "immaculate conception."

When the now-legendary whitepaper,* "Bitcoin: A Peer-to-Peer Electronic Cash System,"[68] was posted to a mailing list for cryptography enthusiasts on October 31, 2008 under the name Satoshi Nakamoto, all clues pointing to personal identity were

---

* A whitepaper is a detailed technical blueprint that clearly explains a project's purpose, design, and implementation for developers and stakeholders.

intentionally obfuscated. Satoshi clearly meant to ensure that the open-source Bitcoin network would never have a leader, chain of command, power structure, or hierarchy.

This cannot be said for any other cryptocurrency. Bitcoin, and Bitcoin alone, is the OG *blockchain*.

In that nine-page paper, Satoshi introduced a way for anyone, anywhere, to send digital "cash" directly to someone else—no bank, no company, no gatekeeper involved—using a public *ledger* secured by math and computing power without needing to trust in a central authority.

↭

*Cryptocurrency* gets its name from *cryptography*—the discipline of protecting digital messages by turning them into scrambled code that only someone with the right key can read. It uses math as a "lock" on data. With digital money, each unit is thus locked in the same way: only the key-holder can send the funds. Because every coin is protected by that lock, the network can safely record transactions, create new coins, and transfer value—all without a central authority.

The term "blockchain" is thrown around quite a bit, so let's put a little more meat on the bones of the concept to better understand its profound significance and to differentiate Bitcoin from all other blockchain protocols.

A blockchain is, as its name suggests, a series of digital "blocks" containing encrypted data, like financial transactions, "chained" together to form a digital ledger.

If that feels like a lot at once, hang tight—we're about to walk through exactly what it all means.

**Figure 8: Blockchain transactions**

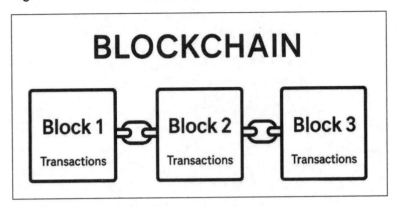

It all began with Bitcoin's first block, known as the Genesis Block. It has an extraordinary message stamped into it—a line pulled straight from the headlines of *The Times*, a London-based newspaper: "The Times 03/Jan/2009 Chancellor on brink of second bailout for banks."

It seems pretty darn clear that Satoshi had the failings of the global financial system in mind when inventing Bitcoin. Its emergence wasn't just coincidental with the banking crisis and the way that the traditional financial system had eroded confidence and bled wealth from the middle class; it was *in response* to it.

And then, as if to seal Bitcoin's destiny as a tool for the common good, Satoshi gave the open-source protocol away and disappeared. Unlike most inventors who guard their creations for profit—or the founders of countless other digital tokens—Satoshi built the masterpiece and vanished.

Satoshi has never touched those original bitcoins, offered the world a system designed to thrive (or fail) purely on its own merits.

⇉

If you're like most of us who find our way to Bitcoin, you're probably surprised to discover how much you'd assumed you understood about money without quite thinking about it.

When people learn that I'm a Bitcoin educator, their first question is usually: What the heck is a bitcoin? Where does it actually come from? Can I hold one?

Unlike coins and dollar bills, a bitcoin has no physicality. You can't actually hold it; like a book you're reading on your phone or a song streaming from Spotify, it's dematerialized. But this doesn't mean it's not real! It just means that its reality is affirmed not in physical space but in cyberspace, on a distributed ledger that's governed by unchangeable laws.

**Bitcoin isn't a physical object, but (for reasons we will unpack in the coming pages) it's considered the "hardest" money ever created. Because its supply is permanently fixed and can't be increased, it resists inflation. Unalterably scarce by design, Bitcoin serves as an unparalleled store of value. This means it has a profound capacity to preserve wealth over time.**

→»

The next few chapters will illustrate Bitcoin's immunity to inflation and explain why it stores value more effectively than any asset in history. We'll also look at Bitcoin's role as a monetary network, often referred to as the *Internet of Money*. Just as no one controls the internet, no one controls Bitcoin! It shifts the power to create and control money from fallible human beings to a set of predefined and unchangeable rules governed by the laws of physics and mathematics.

But first, a clarification: you may have noticed that the word Bitcoin is usually capitalized. With a capital 'B,' Bitcoin refers to the network or payment system—like a highway—that connects people around the world. With a lowercase 'b,' bitcoin refers to the individual digital tokens, like the cars traveling on that highway, carrying value from one person to another.

**Figure 9: Bitcoin network**

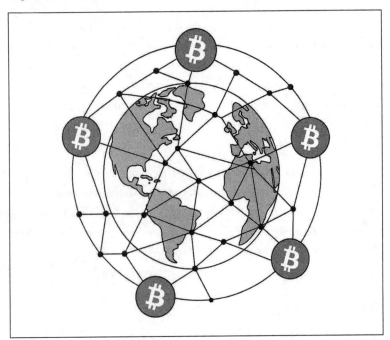

Thinking of the Bitcoin network like the internet helped me visualize it more clearly. The internet is basically a set of rules, or a protocol, that lets computers talk to each other. It's a sort of universal language.

The internet is decentralized: no company or government controls it. It has no headquarters, no central authority, and no governing body. To build applications like email or websites, individuals and companies must use a shared protocol called TCP/IP, which standardizes how information is sent and received across the network.

This protocol works across international borders, enabling computers in any nation to seamlessly interact.

The Bitcoin network operates in a similar way. It's also a decentralized protocol—again, a set of rules without rulers—spoken by all the computers running the Bitcoin software on the network. But while the internet transmits packets of *information* (every email, photo, and video is broken down into tiny data bundles that travel separately and are reassembled upon arrival), the Bitcoin protocol transmits packets of *value* in the form of bitcoins—universal digital tokens that can move securely from one digital wallet to another across the network.

**Figure 10: Packets of information versus packets of value (bitcoins)**

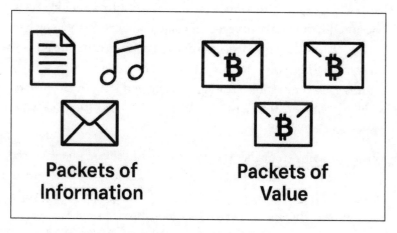

At its core, Bitcoin is a public digital infrastructure, like the internet or a national highway system.

It empowers individuals, companies, and even governments to do what they need to do more efficiently and securely. It's a breakthrough in technology and economics, combining past innovations into a radically new form: a decentralized, digital foundation for storing real value.

To those unfamiliar with its design, Bitcoin might seem similar to other digital assets, but it justifiably occupies a category of its own. While some call it "digital gold" to articulate its role as a store of value, Bitcoin far surpasses this comparison. It represents a new chapter in the history of money—a form of digital capital designed, yes, to store value better than anything we've seen, but also to be resilient, reliable, and—crucially, for our thesis—*accessible to everyone.*

⇻

As we've discussed, money can be thought of as a ledger: a system for tracking who owns what and how much. Just as bookkeepers once used hefty books to record income and expenses line by line, Bitcoin also uses a digital ledger to document every time bitcoins are exchanged. This ledger, in this case the "blockchain", permanently records each transaction, creating a secure and transparent history of all activity on the network. And it's visible to anyone who cares to look.

With Bitcoin, though, there's no need for a bookkeeper. Transactions on the blockchain are verified and recorded automatically by a secure network of computers worldwide running the Bitcoin software. This global ledger—like a shared spreadsheet—is updated whenever a new block of valid transactions is added. Every time bitcoins are sent, a record of the transaction is permanently available to anyone who wants to see it.

A "decentralized global ledger" may sound a bit dry, but its implications border on the infinite. This is where understanding the various pitfalls of all prior forms of money comes into play and why we needed nine chapters to tee up the mind-blowing nature and world-changing potential of Bitcoin.

→»

We've said it before, but it bears repeating: just as there is nobody in charge of the internet, *there's nobody in charge of Bitcoin*. If you take away only a few specific insights from this book, this should undoubtedly be near the top of the list: no individual, group of individuals, company, board, government, or central bank has authority over Bitcoin.

Even Satoshi, Bitcoin's inventor, has no control over the network; the only effect Satoshi's reappearance would have (aside from arousing worldwide curiosity, that is) is on the *price* of bitcoin, and there's no indication whatsoever that Satoshi will resurface.

The importance of this cannot be overstated. Bitcoin is—again, as the title of this book declares—*for everyone,* regardless of nationality, race, gender, or socioeconomic status. It enables all of us to access the public ledger, verify it, and send and receive value to and from anyone in the world using nothing more than a computer and an internet connection.

The Bitcoin network is a permissionless system in which we the users are all peers, which means that nobody is above or below anyone else. And rather than trusting an individual, organization, or government to manage that system properly—with all the risks that come with it, as we saw in the first half of this book—Bitcoin's *consensus-based mechanism* is designed to bypass the need for trust altogether. Though it might sound counterintuitive, this doesn't create mistrust; it makes trust virtually irrelevant.

Ironically, this actually enhances trust in the system itself.

→»

But you may be wondering *how*—how can everyone possibly agree on the state of a digital distributed ledger when no one is in charge?

Let's lift the hood and, like a mechanic examining a car engine, finally begin to check out the nuts and bolts of Bitcoin.

For years, cryptographers—computer scientists specializing in secure communication—had tried to create a true digital cash system native to the internet. As more and more transactions moved online, two seemingly simple tasks remained out of reach: sending digital money directly from one person to another without a bank, payment processor, or other central authority overseeing the process, and preventing the same money from being copied and spent twice.

To understand this double-spending problem, consider this: when you share a photo from your phone, the picture isn't actually transferred—it's duplicated. Both you and the recipient now have a copy, much like using the copy-paste function in a document. With digital cash, this type of duplication is a huge issue. How could you ensure that digital money, once sent, couldn't just be copied and spent again?

In the real world, this exchange is so obvious and straightforward that we barely notice. Let's say you're out to dinner with a group of good friends. One person kindly offers to foot the bill with her credit card; the rest of you can simply pay her back in cash. Easy—this happens all the time! When you hand over your $20 bill, that cash physically leaves your wallet and is tucked into your friend's wallet. The bill clearly can't be in two places at once, so you're both squared away.

Until Bitcoin was invented, this was the digital conundrum: if you were paying your friend for that dinner but the cash never actually left your wallet, then the whole system would immediately break down. Who wouldn't love to spend $20 but keep that $20 at the same time? You can imagine the consequences.

Cryptographers also faced a related problem: how to reach a global agreement on transactions without a central authority to verify and approve them. Without someone in charge, how could everyone on the network trust that recorded transactions were legitimate?

Then came Bitcoin, a groundbreaking solution to both problems at once. Through a combination of advanced cryptography, decentralized consensus, and economic incentives, Bitcoin made it possible to securely transfer digital value across the world without relying on any central authority.

In the next chapter, we'll explore how Bitcoin achieves decentralized consensus—total agreement without a governing body—through a process called *mining*, which carries out a mechanism known as *proof-of-work*. This unique (and, frankly, fascinating) process secures the network and creates new bitcoins on a pre-programmed schedule, ensuring a limited, predictable, and transparent money supply.

-↔»

For now, though, it's important mainly to recognize that with Bitcoin, you don't need Venmo, PayPal, your bank, an airport currency exchange, or any other middleman to access or send your money. You can simply send monetary value *directly* to the recipient, leaving behind a record on the entire network.

There's one more crucial point to note here. Unlike those other services, which track, surveil, and accumulate data with every financial move you make, the Bitcoin network records only that the coins have moved between wallets. There is no other information that can be used to identify, market to, or otherwise use you to further someone else's aims.

Bitcoin doesn't discriminate. It doesn't care whether you are sending a few dollars or a billion dollars. Bitcoin is blind to who you are, how much you're worth, and how you're going to spend it.

**Just like cash**.

→»

Cracking open the puzzle of digital cash is certainly a huge leap forward, but it doesn't fully address the problems with money that we've outlined up to this point. Couldn't digital cash be created even more easily than printed money, with potentially disastrous results?

This is where Bitcoin goes from being a useful new tool to a transformational engineering breakthrough that occupies an asset class all of its own.

Unlike every currency that came before it, Bitcoin's supply is permanently capped—no loopholes, no exceptions.

→»

I'll say that again, because this fact should also be among your top takeaways from this book: *there will only, ever, and for the rest of time be 21 million bitcoins.*

Unlike dollars, gold, real estate, and art, the supply of bitcoins is programmatically and irreversibly fixed. No matter what, 21 million is all we'll ever have: the Bitcoin network will stop production once the last bitcoin has been mined.

And *because it's hard-capped, Bitcoin's supply is immune to inflation.* Citizens, bankers, and government officials can meet in boardrooms, argue until they're red in the face, and stand on their heads: they cannot control or manipulate the supply of bitcoin or change its fixed monetary policy. That policy is reinforced by every single computer running the Bitcoin protocol (we call them nodes— more on that in a bit), and together, by consensus and through the unimpeachable principles of physics and self-interest, they secure the network and make it completely tamper-proof.

→»

The fact that the supply is permanently limited might lead you to believe that Bitcoin is scarce in a way that makes it inaccessible. That it's only for the wealthy, or that you'd have to buy a whole coin to participate. But don't worry—disproving such an idea is the whole point of this book! There's absolutely no need to purchase a whole bitcoin—like pennies to a dollar, each bitcoin is divisible into 100 million units known as *satoshis* (sats for short). You can start to accumulate sats right away!

→»

And once you've bought them, you can rest assured that the integrity of those sats is protected by one of the most secure systems on Earth. Miners, as we'll see in the next chapter, use real-world computing power and energy to create a "wall of encrypted energy," as Michael Saylor refers to it, that makes hacking the Bitcoin network next to impossible, prohibitively expensive, and therefore pretty much unimaginable.

This is where *proof-of-work* (PoW) comes in. Proof-of-work is the process that enables a bunch of computers—spread across the world, operating anonymously, and with no reason whatsoever to trust each other—to verify transactions and thus validate the blocks that'll be permanently added to the blockchain.

Proof-of-work is exactly what it sounds like. You have to put in real computational effort, requiring real-world energy, to earn bitcoins.

All of this happens without the possibility of intervention by a government, bank, or individual trying to manipulate the system for their own gain. Unlike any of the other 175+ currencies in the world—most of them tied to a money printer that fuels inequality from the top down—Bitcoin operates beyond the control of profit-driven banks and corporate interests.

**Stored on a *decentralized blockchain* with encoded rules that apply universally for everyone who holds it, anywhere in the world, Bitcoin is *truly the people's money*.**

↦

Every time a new block of transactions is added to the ledger, it's fused with the prior block in an unbreakable mathematical way. With Bitcoin, the complex process involved with verifying that this information is correct happens approximately every ten minutes and that's where the *nodes* come in. Once the transaction has been verified and accounted for, it is, as we learned above, available as a permanent record for anyone who cares to look.

I always find that visualization really helps to make these complex ideas accessible. One of the best blockchain analogies I've ever encountered was presented on *The Tim Ferriss Show* podcast by Naval Ravikant who built on an idea originally shared by Nick Szabo earlier in the episode.[69]

> If you see a fly in amber and it's got a millimeter of amber around it, that could have been done yesterday or a year ago. But if you see the fly is trapped in a huge block of amber, you know it's been there for a long, long time; it's been accumulating. So, a blockchain is a series of blocks. Each block is a series of computations done by computers all over the world using serious cryptography in a way that's very hard to undo ... each block is like another thin layer of amber, and the chain of blocks represents the depth of that amber; how long that fly has been trapped in, and therefore, you can trust that honest signal.
>
> Anything deep down in the blockchain is mathematically, cryptographically and just economically impossible to undo.

When you think about it that way, the blockchain doesn't seem so much like a chain, but rather more like a series of layers. But I suppose *blocklayers* doesn't exactly roll off the tongue?

Each computer on the Bitcoin network is concretely invested in keeping the system running smoothly, block by block. I run a node. You can run a node. You don't need an MBA, a friend in banking, or even a bank account or credit score. Just a computer.

Once again: *the people's money.*

↠

Earlier, we discussed how our banking system relies entirely on consumer trust. When that trust cracks, even the grandest bank can quickly crumble. At the first sign of trouble, depositors rush to withdraw their money—but as we've learned, thanks to fractional reserve banking, much of that money isn't actually there. The bank has already lent it out in search of profits, and collapse is inevitable.

Unless, that is, the government steps in to bail out the bank.

The relationship between over-leveraged banks and the governments that promise to get them out of trouble is frighteningly similar to a co-dependent marriage between an addict and their spouse: an addict makes mess after mess, and the partner always cleans it up. And this, it seems, is what Satoshi was referring to when that now famous message—"Chancellor on the brink of a second bailout for banks"—was inscribed into the Genesis Block of Bitcoin.

Satoshi created a protocol-driven network of computers that removes this need for trust entirely. Instead of crossing our fingers and hoping that our money will be available to us when we need it, we can rely on a network of computers that, through cryptographic proof, updates the ledger of accounts in real time. *What's there is there, full stop.*

Bitcoiners have a popular shorthand for this reversal: "Don't trust, verify."

To solve the problems that inevitably arise when power becomes consolidated into a small group of individuals or institutions, Bitcoin maintains a distributed ledger of accounts, continuously secured by a vast network of computers all over the world. It becomes literally stronger with each passing hour.

**But don't take my word for it: the proof is in the pudding! Or, in this case, the work stored in the blockchain.**

--->>>

# Chapter 10 Summary

It is deeply symbolic that Bitcoin appeared in 2008—right when governments worldwide were rushing to bail out reckless banks and public trust in central banks was at an all-time low. Bitcoin was designed as the exact opposite of that system: there is no CEO, no board, and no central bank pulling levers behind the scenes. Instead, it runs on open-source code and a fixed rule set—most famously, a hard cap of 21 million coins. Because every transaction is secured by math rather than by human decision-making, Bitcoin is transparent, universally accessible, and immune to the inflationary pressures that come with endlessly printing fiat money.

**Key Takeaway**: Bitcoin is the first form of money with a fixed, unchangeable supply—making it impossible to debase or manipulate politically.

# 11.
# EVERYONE CAN VERIFY BITCOIN'S CODE

**"The work required by the system converts electricity into truthful records."**

HAL FINNEY

---

B Y NOW, I hope it's clear that Bitcoin didn't simply appear out of nowhere to entertain nerdy programmers or create clever new ways to fuel money speculation.

Let's recap: Bitcoin solved an economic and computer science problem that had stumped cryptographers since the 1970s: how to create digital money that couldn't be debased, double-spent and enabled people to exchange value directly—without relying on trust in each other or any intermediary.

While computer scientists had previously attempted to create sound digital money with decentralized control and a rules-based mathematical system, Bitcoin was the first to successfully overcome the technical challenges that had stumped its predecessors.

All great breakthroughs begin with a question. Satoshi Nakamoto wasn't the first to ask, "How can strangers across the world agree on a single, trustworthy digital record without relying on a central authority?"

Others had posed the question, but Satoshi decisively answered it. The solution not only addressed the problem, but also exposed the deep flaws in our financial system while offering a path to fixing them.

↬

Satoshi's achievement wasn't just theoretical: it was practical, elegant, and profoundly egalitarian. At its core lies a system of ownership and verification that relies exclusively on decentralized consensus secured by math and cryptography.

Your bitcoin isn't just numbers on a screen—it represents something revolutionary. A verifiable, finite piece of *digital property* backed by the most powerful computer network on Earth.

**If you own a bitcoin—or even a fraction of one—you hold a share of the only 21 million bitcoins that will ever exist**.

The entire network collectively verifies and attests to your ownership until you decide to transfer your bitcoin to someone else. (We'll cover the logistics of buying and selling bitcoin in Chapter Fifteen.)

For now, think of your bitcoin as sitting in a "digital P.O. box," a secure space on the network to which only you hold the key.

↬

At this point, it's perfectly reasonable to wonder, "If Bitcoin is worth trillions, why can't a clever hacker just rewrite the ledger for their own benefit?" The answer boils down to something you can't fake or shortcut: an open-source ledger secured by real world energy.

Every ten minutes, thousands of specialized computers worldwide engage in a high-stakes race called *proof-of-work mining*. Think of each machine as a sprinter running on electricity instead of muscle—burning watts the way our sprinter burns calories—trying to guess a winning number that will seal the next "page" of Bitcoin's ledger. The first miner to land on that number broadcasts its solution to the world and earns freshly minted bitcoin plus the transaction fees in that block.

Crucially, every wrong guess costs just as much electricity as a right one, so the race is brutally expensive. If someone wanted to tamper with past transactions, they would have to redo not just one race but every race all the way back to the block they want to change—and do it faster than all honest miners combined. The electric bill alone would dwarf the potential reward, turning energy into a near-impenetrable firewall around the ledger.

Running alongside the miners is also a second layer of defense: a global constellation of independent computers known as *nodes*. These machines aren't trying to win any race; their only job is to act as uncompromising referees. Each node keeps a complete copy of the blockchain and checks every proposed block against Bitcoin's rulebook—verifying digital signatures, confirming that no coins are double-spent, and ensuring the block's math is sound.

If even one rule is broken, nodes simply refuse to accept the block, no matter how much electricity was expended to create it. As long as just one honest copy of the ledger exists, the rules hold firm.

Together, miners and nodes form Bitcoin's security loop. Miners pour real energy into locking in each new layer of history, while nodes stand guard to ensure every layer was built correctly.

↦

This self-governing system needs no central authority. With these two interlocking systems, Bitcoin removes financial power dynamics and replaces them with distributed verification and *thermodynamics*—the unforgeable cost of energy—to keep the system honest. Your bitcoin remains safe because breaking the rules would require not only extraordinary computing power, but also a river of electricity so vast that network participants would detect and outspend an attack long before it could succeed.

In other words, Bitcoin turns the traditional financial system on its head.

⇶

In Chapter Ten, we explored how Bitcoin solved the long-standing "double-spend" problem that had plagued attempts at digital cash.

Remember, unlike physical cash, which visibly changes hands when spent, digital cash posed a unique challenge for cryptographers: how could they ensure that a digital token wasn't simply duplicated—like a photo being copied and texted to multiple friends—allowing the same money to be spent more than once?

Before Satoshi's innovation, there was no way to prevent double-spending without relying on a trusted intermediary, like a bank, to keep track of all transactions and ensure no one spent the same money twice.

Satoshi's breakthrough was to create a distributed ledger shared equally among all participants in the network. Every *node* holds a live, synchronized copy of this ledger, updating it in real time. Meanwhile, those *mining computers*—known as ASICs or miners—compete in a reward-driven lottery to solve complex cryptographic puzzles. As with a traditional lottery, miners can't simply print their own tickets and expect to win; their way of "purchasing a ticket" is through expending real-world energy for a chance to add new blocks of transactions to the blockchain and earn the mining reward.

In Bitcoin's system, there's nobody overseeing this process—no person or company running the lottery. Instead, the cryptographic puzzles are intentionally designed to require real-world energy as the entry fee. This energy acts as a verifiable cost of participation, ensuring that miners can't fake their way into the competition or manipulate the results (because you can't print energy any more than you can make it rain!).

This is the *proof-of-work* that keeps the network secure and prevents fraud. It's the ingenious mechanism, grounded in the laws of physics and enforced by a set of unchangeable rules, that enables the competition—and therefore the entire network—to manage itself.

When a miner solves the cryptographic puzzle and earns the right to propose a new block, it broadcasts the block and its solution—including the transactions waiting to be inscribed within it—to the entire Bitcoin network. Every node then independently verifies the block, checking that all transactions follow Bitcoin's consensus rules—confirming, for example, that the sender has sufficient funds to cover their expenditures and that no double-spending has occurred.

No changes to the ledger are finalized until the network reaches agreement on the state of the blockchain. This distributed consensus preserves an immaculate record of transactions.

ASICs and nodes, then, are like two hands locked in an iron grip, creating and reinforcing one of the most secure and resilient networks ever conceived.

**All without anyone in charge**.

↠

With that, let's take a closer look at how this "lottery" actually works.

At any given moment (and as of this writing), approximately one million[70] ASICs—those highly specialized computers designed solely for Bitcoin mining—are racing to solve cryptographic puzzles and earn valuable bitcoin.

If you've ever been asked to "guess a number between one and ten," you have a rough idea of the challenge. But in Bitcoin mining, it isn't a number between one and ten—it's closer to a number between one and the total number of atoms in the known universe. Needless to say, finding the right one takes immense computational effort (and luck!).

Each attempt at solving this puzzle therefore requires significant energy expenditure, which is costly. But the reward is worth it: the computer that guesses correctly gets to add the next batch of transactions to the blockchain. Its owner earns fees from those transactions, but they're really going after a bitcoin reward known as the *block subsidy* or *block reward*—the prize that serves as an economic incentive for miners to keep the network secure and operational.

↦

The rest of the network is also deeply invested in ensuring that every block is accurate and immutable, because the value of Bitcoin depends on its impeccable status as a shared, tamper-proof record of truth. Remember: "Don't trust, verify."

To appreciate the simple elegance of how this is achieved—how the solution to the unfathomably complex "guess a number" puzzle is instantaneously corroborated all over the world, without any help from a judge or referee—it helps to envision a bike lock.

As any would-be bicycle thief knows, guessing a five-digit combination is hard enough, especially under pressure. Now imagine trying to crack a combination so astronomically large that it surpasses human comprehension.

This is essentially what Bitcoin miners are doing: submitting trillions of guesses per second in a high-stakes race to crack the code before anyone else.

Once there's a winner, though, verification is remarkably simple. Just as a bike lock pops open with the correct combination, the winning solution is immediately recognizable and easily confirmed by anyone—in this case, every node on the network. (More on that step in a moment.)

—»

But here's where it gets interesting. If all mining computers were simply trying to crack identical bike locks, you'd expect the results to be predictable: more powerful equipment and increased energy usage would mean the code gets cracked faster and more frequently.

It'd be like digging for gold with a hydraulic pump instead of a shovel: in such a scenario, the supply of bitcoins would be exhausted in no time, disproportionately favoring those with the most advanced technology and deepest pockets. In such a scenario, the entire blockchain would be at risk of being dominated—or even manipulated—by a handful of powerful players.

Preventing this outcome is one of Satoshi's most brilliant achievements, and it brings us to the elegant solution at the heart of Bitcoin mining: the *difficulty adjustment*.

—»

To understand how the difficulty adjustment works, let's take a step back for a moment.

When I described Bitcoin mining as guessing a number somewhere between "one" and "the number of atoms in the known universe," I was introducing the basic idea. But let's refine that analogy.

Miners aren't actually searching for a single, precise number, like cracking a bike lock combination. Instead, they're aiming for a range of acceptable numbers—a constantly shifting target defined by the network.

Yan Pritzker, author of *Inventing Bitcoin*, offers a helpful image to bring this into focus: Bitcoin mining is like throwing darts at an enormous dartboard. The bullseye represents that target range, and to "win," a miner must use a valid cryptographic process to generate a guess (using the data from the newly-forming block *plus* a random number) that lands within the range. The catch? This target range isn't static: it widens or shrinks based on both the amount of computing power currently within the network and how quickly valid guesses are being made.

Whether it's compared to a bike lock with a flexible combination range or a dartboard with a dynamic bullseye, the key takeaway is this: Bitcoin's network is *designed to adapt*.

This built-in adaptability works in real time. If computers are winning too quickly, it means the target is too large, making it too easy to land guesses inside the bullseye. In response, the bullseye automatically shrinks, making it harder to hit and slowing down the pace of wins.

If computers are struggling to find a winning guess, it means the target is too small. In this case, the bullseye expands, making it easier to hit and speeding up the discovery of new blocks.

No matter how many miners join or how much computing power they throw at the problem, the network ensures that new blocks are produced, on average, every ten minutes.

**Bitcoin is like an orchestra that's found a way to keep perfect time without a conductor.**

So here we have millions of contestants on some sort of global game show, all racing to crack an impossibly complex code. There's no host, no moderator, just a million computers relentlessly guessing at astronomical speeds. When one miner finally lands on the winning guess, the rest of the network must agree that it's legitimate.

Now the rubber meets the road: *how* do they verify the winner? How do they know the "bike lock" really popped open?

Validating the winner involves a bit of computer science known as *hashing*. In Bitcoin, hashing serves two purposes: it allows miners to generate their guesses during the competition, and it enables every node on the network to instantly verify whether the winning guess is valid.

### Breakout explanation: hashing

Imagine hashing like making a smoothie. You start with a specific set of ingredients—let's say a banana, strawberries, and yogurt. You blend them together, and the result is a unique smoothie. Once blended, you can't reverse the process to get the original banana or strawberries back; all you have is the final smoothie.

In Bitcoin, the "ingredients" are transaction data, and the "smoothie" is the hash—a unique digital fingerprint created by running that data through a cryptographic formula (the blender). Every tiny change to the ingredients (the data) creates an entirely different smoothie (or hash).

For miners, hashing is like blending millions of smoothies per second, each with slightly different ingredients, hoping to match a secret recipe set by the network. When a miner finally gets the perfect smoothie (winning hash), they share the recipe with the entire network, and everyone else can quickly check to confirm it's the right one.

Of course, the real process is far more precise than making smoothies—hashing is pure math, not subjective judgments about flavor. But the metaphor helps show just how sensitive and irreversible the process really is.

Hashing ensures that the winning guess is valid, secure, and impossible to fake, because no one can tamper with the smoothie once it's blended. That's the magic of hashing: it's incredibly hard to guess the right combination, but incredibly easy for everyone to verify once it's found.

--»

Imagine after 2.3 trillion dart throws, your dart finally lands in the bullseye. Lucky you! On a game show, the host would walk up, inspect your dart, and hand you the prize money on the spot.

But in Bitcoin's system, as we know, there's no host to inspect the dartboard and validate your hit. Instead, every computer on the network leans in, like a global team of math teachers, and asks you to "show your work."

If you legitimately won—by "blending the perfect smoothie," so to speak—each computer can instantly verify it, earning you the right to record transactions into the next block on the blockchain.

Any attempt to cheat will be immediately obvious and result in the automatic rejection of your claim. All the energy you'd spent mining will have been wasted. In this system of "rules without rulers," there's no loophole, no workaround, nobody to whom you can plead your case. You either follow the rules, validate your work, and earn the reward, or you burn money on electricity and walk away empty-handed.

-↬↬-

This is the essence of Bitcoin's proof-of-work. It's a system that keeps the network secure by making cheating both costly and impractical. Just as you and I can't print money at home to pay off our credit card bills, miners must invest real resources—electricity, computing power, and hardware—to be financially rewarded. By ensuring that every guess comes with a tangible cost, Bitcoin turns real-world energy expenditure into the foundation of its strength and security. As we'll explore in Chapter Twelve, where we unpack criticisms of Bitcoin's energy use, this requirement isn't a flaw, it's the feature that makes the system trustworthy and tamper-resistant.

-↬↬-

So *that's* what the mining computers are up to! They're solving complex puzzles and competing for block rewards. But, as we noted at the start of this chapter, they only account for *half* of the Bitcoin ecosystem.

This is where *nodes* come in: while blocks are being mined, nodes continuously verify and secure every transaction recorded on the ledger. In fact, it's thanks to nodes that Bitcoin can rightfully claim the mantle of "the people's money."

A node is simply a computer running the open-source Bitcoin software while storing the entire blockchain. Installing one is about as straightforward as downloading a desktop app—if you can set up Microsoft Word, you can spin up a node—so anyone with a modest computer and internet connection can join the network.

Picture a node as a smart security camera. Instead of watching a single doorway, it peers into every corner of Bitcoin's ledger. Each node independently validates every transaction and every block, line by line, against Bitcoin's unchanging rulebook. No payment or block reward becomes part of the permanent record unless thousands of these digital inspectors reach unanimous consensus that it obeys the rules.

In this way, nodes form a worldwide chorus of truth-tellers, continuously auditing the work of miners and preserving the integrity of the entire blockchain.

The fact that everyone can verify the entire system from their own machine is the key to Bitcoin's decentralization. This truth is revealed in Bitcoin's design: in order to make sure that absolutely anyone, anywhere can run a node and help keep the network honest, block size was deliberately set at a level everyday computers could manage.

If blocks were too large, the hardware requirements to run a node—storage, processing power, and bandwidth—would become prohibitively expensive. This would naturally limit participation to those with significant financial resources, concentrating power in the hands of the wealthy and undermining Bitcoin's core principles of decentralization and universal access.

Instead, Bitcoin's lightweight design allows anyone with an internet connection and a modest, affordable device to download the entire blockchain, validate transactions, and secure the network from home.

Imagine if ordinary people could "look over the shoulder" of our traditional financial system and see what the banks are *really* up to. At the moment, the most consequential decisions—decisions that affect all of us, like how much money to print—happen behind closed doors, among a small group of people with varying interests and incentives.

Ordinary people have no way to challenge (or even see!) what they're doing.

Now imagine a system where every monetary action is public—where anyone, anywhere, can verify the rules are being followed, and no one can secretly change them.

Bitcoin is that system. And it's working.

—»»

A common criticism of Bitcoin is its perceived "slowness" due to the ten-minute intervals between those blocks. As we now know, that timing is determined by the difficulty adjustment. But this isn't a weakness; it's one of Bitcoin's most important features. This deliberate pace also ensures that people all over the world can run their nodes using modest household computers.

What Bitcoin lacks in speed, it more than makes up for in resilience and global reach. From California to Argentina, Thailand to Italy, individuals are securing the Bitcoin network on devices no more powerful than a home desktop. And as we'll explore in the next chapter, Bitcoin's layered architecture allows faster payment networks to be built *on top of* its base layer, combining the security that comes with accessible, widespread verification with near-instant transaction capacity on the front end (say, if you want to buy a coffee!).

So the next time someone criticizes Bitcoin for being "slow," you'll know they're overlooking the very design choices that make it one of the most secure and decentralized financial systems in history.

—»»

It probably comes as no surprise to learn that I've chosen to run a node myself. I like to think of the node system as a kind of "neighborhood watch" for the Bitcoin network: the more people monitoring what's happening, the stronger and more protected the network becomes.

Running a node isn't required to use Bitcoin, and there's no compensation for doing so.

However, once people understand how Bitcoin offers an alternative to our inflationary financial system—one where your savings aren't quietly eroded—they often feel compelled to contribute. Running a node strengthens the network and boosts its resilience and transparency. It's a gratifying part of supporting a system based on truth, not trust.

↦

Now that we understand the basic dynamic between nodes and miners—with nodes keeping the network honest and miners racing to add new blocks and earn financial rewards—it's time to zoom in on the *prizes* (made up of freshly minted bitcoin and the transaction fees that accompany their newly minted block) those miners are earning.

In other words, it's time to see what all the fuss is about!

The block reward, also known as the *block subsidy*, is the primary incentive for mining bitcoin. This reward operates on a predetermined schedule built directly into Bitcoin's code, ensuring fairness and predictability.

When Bitcoin was launched in 2009, the block reward was set at 50 bitcoins per block. If you think back to the Genesis Block— the very first block mined—it was Satoshi Nakamoto who earned this initial reward. At that time, those 50 bitcoins weren't worth anything—Bitcoin was still unknown to the world, save for Satoshi and a handful of cryptographers, so there was zero demand for the new digital token.

While 50 bitcoins are worth an extraordinary sum today, it's important to understand why Satoshi set the reward at that level. It was the early days: few people knew about Bitcoin, even fewer cared, and only a tiny group was willing to expend any energy at all to mine it. At the same time, the puzzle was pretty easy to solve: the bullseye was massive, and the computational effort required to land inside of it was minimal.

In essence, early miners were rewarded handsomely for their curiosity and willingness to participate in a grand experiment. And because bitcoins had no real-world value at the time, the incentive had to be significant enough to justify the effort. At that point, bitcoin really was a sort of "magic internet money."

⇶

In fact, a year after Satoshi released the White Paper, two crypto enthusiasts transacted in bitcoin "in the real world" for the very first time. A programmer named Laszlo Hanyecz famously paid 10,000 bitcoins for two Papa John's pizzas!

At today's prices, those pizzas would cost more than a billion dollars—arguably the most expensive meal in history. But this transaction wasn't about the food; it was a monumental moment for Bitcoin. For the first time, Bitcoin was used as a *medium of exchange* in a commercial transaction, proving it could, indeed, function as digital money.

⇶

That moment showed that Bitcoin did, indeed, have real-world potential. But to preserve its long-term value, Satoshi made a crucial design choice. Rather than setting a fixed mining reward (keeping it at, say, 50 bitcoins per block), Satoshi programmed a diminishing reward schedule into Bitcoin's design. Every 210,000 blocks— roughly every four years—the block reward would diminish by *half*, in a scheduled event aptly referred to as "the *halving*."

Why does this matter? Because it ensures that Bitcoin's issuance schedule follows a predictable and finite trajectory, ultimately capping the total supply at 21 million bitcoins. The halving is a critical feature of the Bitcoin incentive structure, mimicking the natural scarcity of resources like gold while also creating a built-in payoff for early adoption.

This tapered, disinflationary schedule is, again, highly purposeful: it encourages robust mining activity early on, but winds down as the network matures (and payment layers continue to develop above the base protocol), supporting Bitcoin's growth as a medium of exchange.

As the block reward approaches zero—many, many years from now—miners will become incentivized primarily by the transaction fees associated with a streamlined global payment network and its endless hum of activity.

The block reward may shrink with every halving, but Bitcoin's price and adoption rate have historically grown as people continue to strengthen it with their investment of real-world energy, offsetting the consequences of that reduction. This elegant design ensures that Bitcoin mining remains a worthwhile pursuit, even as the block reward decreases over time.

→»

The block reward has undergone several halvings since Satoshi mined the Genesis Block. In 2012, the reward dropped from 50 bitcoins to 25, then to 12.5, 6.25, and finally 3.125, where it stands at the time of this writing.

## Chart 5: Block reward and halving

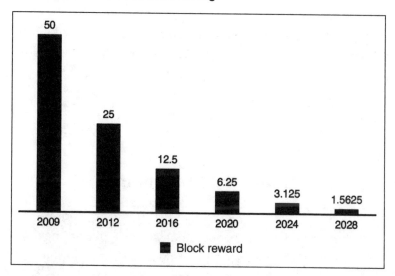

Source: Satoshi Nakamoto, "Bitcoin: A Peer-to-Peer Electronic Cash System" (2008).

It can be pretty shocking to realize that nearly 20 million of the total 21 million bitcoins have already been mined in just over 15 years.

Even more astonishing is the timeline ahead: mining the final 1.2 million bitcoins will take until approximately the year 2140, a date that feels almost impossibly distant. This gradual and predictable distribution schedule is one of Bitcoin's most ingenious features, carefully balancing scarcity, incentive, and long-term sustainability.

When the last bitcoin is mined, the 21 million bitcoins in circulation will represent all the bitcoin that'll ever be created for the rest of eternity!

↦

At this point, calling Bitcoin "magic internet money" is like calling math itself "magical." Just because you can't hold a mathematical equation in your hands doesn't mean it isn't real. Bitcoin may have started as an unproven experiment, but it has since evolved into a globally distributed network anchored to an immutable foundation that nobody, no matter how powerful, can manipulate.

That foundation is energy itself.

⇾⇥

# Chapter 11 Summary

Bitcoin solved a major computer science puzzle: how to create digital money without needing a trusted third party. This breakthrough is accomplished through *proof-of-work*, which requires miners to expend real-world energy to solve complex cryptographic puzzles as a way of securing the network and earning new coins. Bitcoin is therefore tied to physical reality—electricity—rather than human promises. The coins are issued, by design, along a predictable schedule that relies on a *difficulty adjustment* to keep a predictable pace. This will continue until the entire supply of 21 million bitcoins has been mined by 2140.

**Key Takeaway**: Bitcoin anchors its value to real-world energy and unbreakable math—creating a digital asset with true scarcity enforced by physics, not politics.

# 12.
# EVERYONE NEEDS ENERGY

**"Energy is the currency of the universe."**

EMILY MAROUTIAN

O NE OF THE first things people bring up when they hear about my interest in Bitcoin is its energy use.

I get it—it was one of my earliest questions and concerns, too. We all want a healthy, thriving planet with clean air and water, vibrant oceans and forests, and fertile soil to grow nutritious food.

But most people don't fully understand why Bitcoin consumes energy. They don't know what problem it's solving, or how its energy use is fundamentally different from other energy-intensive industries. Bitcoin isn't simply burning energy for the sake of it. It's securing a monetary network that can't be cheated, manipulated, or controlled by any single government, corporation, or individual.

The criticism that Bitcoin mining is a "waste of energy" stems from a misunderstanding, not just of Bitcoin itself, but of the increasingly important (and positive!) role Bitcoin mining is poised to play in the global energy economy. Far from being a pointless drain on resources, Bitcoin mining is emerging as a powerful force for innovation, efficiency, and even environmental stewardship.

⇥»

**Bitcoin is not a company seeking profit. It's an open-source solution to the inflationary chaos caused by a broken monetary system.**

When critics point to Bitcoin's energy consumption, they often overlook that bigger picture. As Chart 6 illustrates, Bitcoin's energy use pales in comparison to industries that consume far more energy with far less scrutiny—even those that *add* to our problems rather than solving them.

A quick glance at the data shows that Bitcoin's use of energy is remarkably small compared with industries like tourism, fashion, or tobacco. The tobacco industry, for instance, not only consumes more energy than Bitcoin, but also contributes to the growing strain on healthcare systems—an industry already using an estimated 3,716 TWh annually (only slightly less than global tourism).[71] But people rarely think about that industry in energy terms.

Investment strategist Lyn Alden puts it all into perspective: Bitcoin is responsible for *"less than 0.1% of the world's energy consumption."*[72] Even if Bitcoin scales massively to become a widely adopted global asset class, Alden argues that its energy usage would still represent only a few tenths of a percentage point. This is essentially a "rounding error as far as global energy usage is concerned."

## Chart 6: Cambridge Bitcoin electricity consumption index (MtCO2e per year)

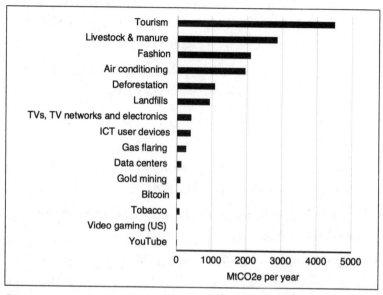

Source: University of Cambridge, "Cambridge Bitcoin Electricity Consumption Index," www.ccaf.io.

"When scientists estimate that the world uses a certain amount of energy in a given year," she continues, "they can easily be off by a couple percentage points in either direction, let alone a couple tenths of a percent."

To drive home the point, Alden adds that simply turning off unused—unused!—electronics 10% more often would save more energy than the entire Bitcoin network consumes.[73]

Why do we forgive so many other industries for their energy consumption—not to mention the legacy financial system itself—but focus so single-mindedly on the portion of the energy pie that Bitcoin occupies?

I think it's because most people are unaware of all the *good* that Bitcoin achieves.

⇢⇢

What's more, Bitcoin doesn't just use *less* energy than we've been led to believe, it can actively contribute to a *more* sustainable and efficient energy future. As we'll explore:

- It *helps harness renewable energy sources*, including those that would otherwise go to waste or remain stranded.

- It *expands access to reliable energy* in regions that have long suffered without it.

- It *enhances grid stability* by balancing supply and demand, making energy systems more efficient.

- It *reduces environmentally harmful overconsumption* by promoting long-term savings.

Not bad for a form of tamper-proof, incorruptible digital money that enables us to save, transact directly with one another, and restore fairness and integrity to the global financial system.

⇢⇢

But let's widen the lens even further: no matter our opinions or feelings about Bitcoin, one truth remains undeniable: *the universe is made up entirely of matter and energy.*

The law of conservation of energy tells us that we can't create or destroy energy. We can, however, decide how best to use it to make life better, richer, and more comfortable. The central question isn't, "Is using energy good or bad?" Evidence shows that access to energy is strongly correlated with human flourishing, including improved health and higher quality of life.[74]

The real question becomes: *how can we best harness the available energy* to improve life not only for ourselves, but also for people around the world?

⇢

As we discussed in the last chapter, Bitcoin's security is rooted in energy and physics. You can't conjure bitcoin out of nowhere (or print it at will) when it's convenient. Each block is created and secured by a decentralized network of computers, using energy to cryptographically link it to the previous block—all the way back to Satoshi Nakamoto's Genesis Block.

This impenetrable fortress, built and reinforced by the cumulative energy and computational effort invested into it, will remain secure as long as computers continue running the Bitcoin software.

This is because it's built on real, verifiable energy. Its resilience doesn't rely on trust in an institution or individual, but on the immense computational power required to maintain and validate every block of transactions. As we learned in prior chapters, each time energy is expended to secure a new block, an indelible record is added to the blockchain—*proof* that the *work* was actually done and the integrity of the network upheld.

Imagine the blockchain like a bodybuilder. Every rep in the gym and every nutritious meal becomes part of their physical form, a tangible result of effort and energy. Similarly, every block added to the Bitcoin network represents that cumulative investment of real-world energy, permanently embedded in its digital structure and maintained by ongoing effort.

⇢

As we saw in Chapter Eleven, Bitcoin miners are specialized machines charged with one task: mining bitcoin. All they need is an energy source and a connection to the network. Their unique advantage? They can operate anywhere energy is available, including places where power would otherwise go to waste. They're like a mechanical Pac-Man, forever munching cheap energy to solve those puzzles, earn the block reward, and reap as much profit as possible.

Many of us share legitimate concerns about our energy future. While energy itself is abundant (as one *Forbes* headline put it, "We Could Power The Entire World By Harnessing Solar Energy From 1% Of The Sahara"), our ability to capture, store, and distribute renewable energy at scale remains a major challenge. Technologies like batteries are advancing, but not quickly enough to meet the growing global demand.

Bitcoin's energy consumption often draws criticism from environmental advocates. On the surface, it might seem like Bitcoin's energy usage is inherently wasteful or incompatible with sustainability goals.

However, Bitcoin mining is increasingly recognized—even by institutions like the World Bank[75]—as a potential ally in building a more efficient and resilient global energy system.

Over the last decade or so, investment in renewables has skyrocketed. In many cases, we're not facing a shortage of energy production, we're facing a storage problem. As we just alluded to, batteries aren't yet capable of storing meaningful quantities of that excess energy. When there's nowhere for surplus energy to go, it's often *curtailed*— that is, production is deliberately reduced or wasted because the grid can't absorb it.

Well, that energy had no place to go until now.

**Bitcoin miners are well-suited to consume energy that would be otherwise wasted, because it's often the *cheapest energy available*, and low energy costs are essential for mining profitability.**

Renewable sources around the world—hydropower in the Himalayas, solar farms in West Texas, geothermal wells in Kenya—

are already being used to mine bitcoin, turning stranded or excess power into economic value.

There are sustainable, under-utilized energy sources all over the world just waiting to be harnessed.

In California alone, so much solar energy was curtailed in 2022 that the wasted power could have supported 200,000 homes for an entire year, according to the World Economic Forum.[76] Imagine the economic and environmental potential if that surplus energy had been harnessed productively.

⇻

Many critics often fail to recognize the waste—immeasurably costly in terms of asset bubbles, malinvestment, and instability—of an economy operating without hard money. Bitcoin not only addresses those economic outcomes that we're experiencing all the time, it also creates real incentives in the physical world, particularly in the field of energy, that are uniquely suited to improving the energy grid we all rely on.

That grid is a remarkable feat of engineering. Every time we flip a light switch or open a refrigerator, a finely tuned system of scientific, economic, and logistical processes kicks into action. Supply and demand must be perfectly balanced in real time—a delicate task managed by energy producers, distributors, and grid operators.

This balance becomes even harder to strike with energy sources like wind and solar, which produce power inconsistently. The sun isn't always shining and the winds aren't always blowing. Surprisingly, having *too much* energy on the grid can be just as bad as having *too little*; both situations can cause instability, inefficiency, and even blackouts.

You can think of the grid like an engine: too little oil, and it seizes up; too much oil, and it overflows and breaks down.

**Bitcoin miners act as a flexible pressure release valve. They can quickly turn on or off, soaking up excess energy when there's too much and powering down when the grid needs more capacity elsewhere.**

This unique ability makes them a valuable tool for keeping the grid stable and efficient.

⇥

Energy cost isn't the *only* factor for mining Bitcoin, but it's among the most critical.[77] When demand (and cost) for energy is high, miners can power down. When demand drops and energy becomes cheap, they fire back up. This natural alignment creates a perfect partnership between Bitcoin mining and grid efficiency.

It's no surprise, then, that places like the UAE,[78] Iceland, Texas, and Quebec—where renewables are particularly abundant—have actively welcomed Bitcoin miners to help stabilize their grids.[79]

For anyone who supports renewable energy, Bitcoin's role in balancing and strengthening energy infrastructure should be seen as a win.

⇥

Bitcoin mining doesn't just prevent energy from being wasted, either. It actively supports the growth of renewable energy projects by improving their economic viability.

In regions with mismatched energy supply and demand, miners act as flexible energy consumers. This adaptability helps smooth out the wrinkles in energy grids, making renewables more reliable and sustainable, and removing the need for taxpayer-funded subsidies.

Talk about a win-win!

⇥

But not all energy challenges are about balancing supply and demand on the grid. Sometimes, the problem isn't excess energy—it's *stranded* energy.

Across the globe, abundant energy sources sit unused because they're too remote or too costly to access. These overlooked opportunities often go to waste simply because there's no viable way to capture their value.

If you've ever played Pac-Man, you know the feeling of that one stubborn dot left in the corner of the screen. These pockets of energy are like that last dot! They're isolated, hard to reach, and impossible to connect to the rest of the grid.

Take landfills—an environmental challenge on multiple fronts. Landfills release methane, a greenhouse gas over 80 times more potent, in terms of warming the atmosphere, than carbon dioxide. Methane is also indirectly responsible for over a million premature respiratory deaths around the world each year.[80] According to the EPA, landfills accounted for 17% of total U.S. methane emissions in 2022.[81]

Capturing and repurposing methane is an appealing idea in theory, but the cost of building infrastructure to introduce methane into energy grids is prohibitively high. With thousands of landfills scattered across the U.S., most methane simply escapes into the atmosphere unchecked, year after year, with disastrous consequences.

Enter Bitcoin mining. Innovative companies are now deploying Bitcoin miners to intercept the release of landfill methane, convert it into electricity, and turn it into a revenue stream. The end result? Less methane in our atmosphere, less environmental harm, and a new way to monetize what was previously poisonous waste. Truly, one man's trash becomes another man's treasure.

And the same goes for the natural gas that comes along with oil extraction. With no cost-effective way to capture and transport this gas, oil companies often burn it off in a process called flaring—a controlled burn that still releases harmful emissions, including methane.

But companies are quickly realizing that natural gas (150 billion cubic meters in 2022 alone—enough to power entire countries!) could be harnessed for mining bitcoin, creating revenue from waste, and drastically reducing emissions. This practice has also earned recognition from the World Bank.

→»

Beyond addressing environmental waste and grid efficiency, Bitcoin mining holds another profound promise: the potential to bring electricity to communities that have long lived without it.

While energy abundance is taken for granted in many parts of the world, billions of people still suffer from "energy poverty"[82]—a lack of reliable access to electricity that hinders economic growth, education, healthcare, and overall quality of life.

Bitcoin's capacity to harness stranded energy isn't just good news for environmental advocates—it's life-changing for people in regions like sub-Saharan Africa, where electricity remains scarce or unreliable. About 43% of the population lacks access to any electricity at all,[83] and even urban areas often face routine blackouts and unstable energy grids. These regions are abundant in natural resources like sunlight, wind, and hydropower, but they lack the financial infrastructure and investment needed to harness these resources effectively.

Such energy poverty isn't just an inconvenience; it's a devastating barrier to progress. Without reliable energy, agriculture can't scale, clean water is harder to access, healthcare systems remain fragile, and schools can't function effectively. As Habitat for Humanity explains, "Insufficient energy usually translates into the impossibility to develop agriculture and manufacturing, thus keeping the poorest countries trapped in a vicious circle: they cannot afford the energy that can drive them out of poverty."[84]

Bitcoin mining has the potential to break this cycle. By providing a financial incentive to build and maintain energy infrastructure, miners can make it economically viable to bring power to remote or underserved areas. Instead of waiting for governments or international organizations to bridge the gap, communities can leverage Bitcoin mining as a catalyst to kickstart their energy independence.

→»

Alex Gladstein of the Human Rights Foundation has spent his career analyzing the matrix of interlocking problems associated with the effects of currency and energy access on human rights and global flourishing. He is convinced that Bitcoin plays an essential role in incentivizing energy development in underserved areas and helping spark economic growth and opportunity in these communities.

In Malawi, for example, only 15% of the population has access to electricity,[85] despite the country's rich hydro-energy potential. Previous attempts to harness this resource for rural electrification failed due to high costs and logistical challenges. In 2023, a Bitcoin mining company stepped in with a focus on grid stability, affordable power, and increased connections. By using hydro-energy to power mining operations, they not only turned a profit but also improved energy access for the local community—all without relying on foreign aid.

Similar success stories are emerging globally, from Bhutan[86] to Uruguay.[87] In Norway, Bitcoin mining facilities repurpose their excess heat to support fish farming operations and warm local community buildings.[88] In Congo, a chocolate factory uses hydroelectric power to mine bitcoin, reinvesting earnings into wages, infrastructure, and cocoa bean processing.[89]

These projects demonstrate Bitcoin's potential to turn untapped energy resources into economic growth and community empowerment—and they make me incredibly hopeful.

⟶⟶

The arrival of electricity in remote communities isn't just a technical achievement—it's life-changing, especially for women. Without reliable electricity, basic tasks like cooking and washing clothes become all-consuming, leaving little time for education, employment, or leisure.

As a World Bank representative in Bolivia observed, energy access reduces the time women spend on domestic labor, enabling them to pursue paid work, education, and entrepreneurial opportunities.[90]

When we consider that *three billion people worldwide use less electricity in a year than an average American refrigerator,*[91] it's clear that addressing global energy inequality is urgent. And Bitcoin may be one of the most powerful tools we have.

⟶⟶

In the U.S., the problems Bitcoin solves aren't always immediately obvious. Again, we often criticize Bitcoin's energy use while overlooking the vast energy consumption of systems we rely on daily—banks, data centers powering our email and cloud servers, and other industries depicted earlier in Chart 6. We benefit from these systems without questioning their environmental impact because their value feels self-evident.

It's also worth recognizing that our experience of energy abundance shapes our perspective. In most parts of the U.S., we can afford to debate fossil fuels versus renewables because we have consistent access to both. But this lens can sometimes obscure Bitcoin's potential to address pressing global issues.

—»

At first glance, Bitcoin might seem like an added burden on an already strained energy system—a little like those tiny birds, called *oxpeckers*, that cling to the backs of rhinoceroses. You might think they're little more than pests, freeloading on the massive creatures they ride.

But the oxpecker isn't a burden at all. It feeds on parasites, warns the rhino of approaching danger, and keeps its host healthier and safer in return. Its Swahili name, *askari wa kifaru*, translates to "the rhino's guard."[92]

Bitcoin is like those oxpeckers. Far from being a burden on the energy grid, it actively *serves* our energy systems—balancing grids, monetizing stranded and wasted energy, and incentivizing renewable development.

—»

Like the rhino, we all want to be comfortable. In fact, the history of human innovation could be summed up as a pursuit of more comfortable, secure, and fulfilling lives. Most innovations—from modern medicine to clean water, from washing machines to video calls with loved ones halfway around the world—depend on energy.

At every level of society, from the necessary (food systems) to the lovely (art, music, film), energy is the source from which all else springs.

**Bitcoin doesn't steal from a limited energy pool, it optimizes it. It identifies friction points in our global energy systems, smooths them out, and makes them more efficient.**

Like the oxpecker tending to its rhino, Bitcoin can also be light-footed, purposeful, and beneficial.

–»

As energy continues to flow into the Bitcoin network, its security and resilience will only grow stronger. But no amount of energy, no matter how vast, will ever create more bitcoin. Remember: its supply is fixed.

This means that Bitcoin stands as an unprecedented store of value, powered by real-world energy.

If we can naturally incentivize renewable energy development, lift millions of people out of energy poverty, and fix our money system—all while streamlining a costly and inefficient global payment network, as we'll explore in the next chapter—then it's hard to argue that Bitcoin isn't worth every watt.

–»

## Chapter 12 Summary

Bitcoin's energy usage—less than 0.1% of global energy consumption—is not only minimal compared to other industries, it's also poised to help *solve* many of our energy-related problems. Bitcoin mining can operate anywhere, anytime, often using otherwise wasted energy like flared methane or surplus solar. It also helps strengthen and stabilize energy grids by balancing supply and demand, all while securing an efficient monetary system that requires no other infrastructure to function.

**Key Takeaway**: Bitcoin's use of energy is not a waste, it's a source of financial resilience.

# 13.
# EVERYONE CAN CONNECT TO THE INTERNET OF MONEY

**"This 'telephone' has too many shortcomings to be seriously considered as a means of communication."**

WESTERN UNION INTERNAL MEMO, 1876

---

N EW TECHNOLOGIES HAVE a way of being dismissed, sometimes fiercely, before they're embraced.

When electricity was introduced, critics feared it would set houses ablaze. Early cars were mocked as noisy, unreliable toys compared to trusty horses. Airplanes? Everyone said they were impossible, until the Wright brothers took off. Even the internet, now woven into every corner of our lives, was once dismissed.

"Man won't fly for a million years."
— *The New York Times*, December 8, 1903

"Internet 'may be just a passing fad as millions give up on it'."
— *Daily Mail*, December 5, 2000

In 1994, on one of my favorite morning news programs, anchor Katie Couric asked in a now-viral clip,[93] "Can you explain what internet is?" Her co-anchors were all comically perplexed by the new technology. Some experts even said that the internet's impact on the economy "would be no greater than the fax machine."[94]

Those predictions certainly haven't aged well. The internet has indisputably transformed the way we communicate, send information, and conduct business all over the world.

→»

Bitcoin is no different. Like any truly revolutionary new technology, it's been misunderstood, ridiculed, and dismissed as a speculative toy or a tech fad. But just like those groundbreaking innovations before it, Bitcoin isn't just a new tool. It's a new paradigm.

In many ways, Bitcoin is the *Internet of Money*—a decentralized network designed to move value as seamlessly and borderlessly as the internet moves information.

If, in the 1990s, you could have bought a share of the internet itself—a token representing ownership in the very foundation of the World Wide Web—it would have been one of the greatest investments of all time. While you can't buy a piece of the internet, you *can* buy bitcoin.

→»

As we mentioned earlier, the internet's ability to "dematerialize" goods and services has put books, music, and even entire libraries into our pockets, instantly accessible to anyone connected to the web. It has delivered knowledge, culture, and entertainment to billions of people worldwide on an unprecedented scale.

It has changed our lives so quickly and so radically that it's sometimes hard to even recognize the transformation. If you're reading this book on a Kindle or listening to it on Audible, for example, you're doing something that would have been quite literally inconceivable to most people just a few decades ago.

Pressing a button and having physical products show up at your door? Like something out of a sci-fi novel. Streaming nearly every TV show and movie ever made, on demand?

Unthinkable.

Bitcoin entered the world under a similar cloud of doubt and confusion—one that still lingers in many circles today. If the transformative potential of the internet was so drastically underestimated, it stands to reason that the Internet of Money—a decentralized digital financial network—would also be initially misunderstood.

Like language or electricity (or money!), the internet is so deeply integrated into our lives that we rarely stop to consider what it actually is. Stepping back to examine its core features can help us better understand why Bitcoin, too, is such a monumental breakthrough.

At its core, the internet is a *network*—it's right there in the name! What makes this network extraordinary is its decentralized nature. There's no single point of control, and therefore, no single point of failure. While access might be disrupted in certain regions or restricted by specific governments, these are exceptions, not the rule. In essence, the internet is *global*—a vast, resilient system connecting billions of devices worldwide.

Importantly, the internet isn't governed by any single person, company, or institution. Instead, it operates according to *protocols*—standardized rules that ensure all computers on the network can communicate seamlessly. As we touched on in Chapter Ten, the primary protocol behind the internet is TCP/IP (Transmission Control Protocol/Internet Protocol). This protocol acts as a universal language, enabling computers across continents to exchange information reliably and efficiently.

↣

But a worldwide language only works if everyone uses it!

Imagine that you and your best friend were the only ones who knew about the internet when it first came out. Interesting, perhaps, but certainly not life-changing.

But if you each found a way to share it with others, who shared it, in turn, with their friends and family, pretty soon—as anyone who's forwarded a meme or had a viral song stuck in their heads undoubtedly knows—the system will have spread like wildfire.

As more people join, the network becomes increasingly powerful. According to the World Bank, the digital economy has been growing 2.5 times faster than the physical world economy,[95] a trend that shows no signs of abating.

That phenomenon is known as the *network effect*.

↣

The network effect doesn't just make Bitcoin more valuable—it makes it *more secure*. As we've covered in prior chapters, the more people who participate in the network, the harder it becomes to attack or manipulate.

In the early days, when Bitcoin was still small and relatively unknown, vulnerabilities might have existed. But today, the sheer size, distribution, and computational power of the network have transformed Bitcoin into that "wall of encrypted energy."

And yet, one of the most common questions people still ask when learning about Bitcoin is: how can something digital truly be tamper-proof? How can we be sure no one—no government, no rogue actor—can take it over or shut it down?

It all comes back, once again, to Bitcoin's decentralized design—powered by that globally distributed network of participants—which gives it unparalleled resilience against attacks. **No single point of failure exists because no one controls the system**.

As we explored earlier, any attempt to manipulate or breach the blockchain would either be rejected outright by the network or rendered irrelevant as the blockchain adapts and reroutes around the issue. This self-correcting mechanism ensures that every block added to the chain is cryptographically verified and agreed upon by the majority of participants.

At this point, experts widely agree: the Bitcoin network has reached such an immense level of computational density and distributed consensus that a successful large-scale attack is effectively impossible.

**In short, Bitcoiners sleep well at night**.

→»

Lyn Alden uses Wikipedia as a way to illustrate network effects—and to show how nearly impossible it is for competitors to catch up once something reaches a certain level of ubiquity. Lyn writes:

> I could technically copy Wikipedia (all of the data can fit on a thumb drive) and try to host it on my website as Lynpedia. Would I be a real challenge to Wikipedia's traffic if I did? Of course not. Even if I copy the full text, I can't copy the hundreds of millions of links on countless websites pointing to the real Wikipedia, the top search rankings and massive

server capacity that Wikipedia has, or the community of people that continually update Wikipedia. It would be a non-serious competitor.[96]

Like Lyn, I might be interested in starting a new company called "NatalieBook," and try to recruit users to my new platform for social engagement. My mom and best friend would definitely join, but I'm pretty sure Mark Zuckerberg wouldn't bat an eyelash.

Because of the network effect, Lynpedia and NatalieBook would both fail spectacularly.

⟶⟶

Similarly, even the most brilliant person on Earth couldn't succeed in inventing a new protocol capable of replacing our current internet infrastructure. It wouldn't matter if the new protocol was technically superior, because the TCP/IP protocol has established an irreversible dominance.

The internet's protocol (IP) allows us to send packets of information across the world—*information over IP*. This protocol revolutionized communication and society at large (though it wasn't great news for mail carriers and bike messengers). In much the same way, Bitcoin's protocol allows us to send packets of value directly to one another—*money over IP*—through an open-source network that, in many ways, revives something we've almost lost completely.

Think about it: in ancient times, trading was simple and direct. People exchanged goods or money freely, without asking anyone for permission. There were no middlemen, no gatekeepers—just two parties offering something of value—whether it was beads, shells, or early coins. They were making trades as equals.

Today, things are far more complicated. We can't just send money online directly to someone else. Instead, we must navigate a tangled web of middlemen, including banks, payment processors, and third-party financial institutions.

Each step comes with fees, approvals, and oversight. We need permission just to open an account! Every transaction is monitored, our financial data is harvested and sold, and countless toll-takers claim their cut along the way.

→»

Why should it be this way? Why does a whole industry need to profit from my decision to use something that belongs to me?

It's as if we're constantly requesting permission to send our own money—jumping through hoops, paying extra fees, and giving up our privacy. Enter Bitcoin: money that flows directly, peer-to-peer, without hidden fees or the need for permission.

There's an absurdly convoluted web of intermediaries involved in modern financial transactions. From the moment you swipe your credit card, tap your phone, or click "send payment," a cascade of middlemen springs into action. Each layer represents a different player in the payment ecosystem: issuing banks, acquiring banks, credit card networks, payment processors, fraud detection services, and data analytics firms all take a cut or extract value along the way.

For the last 50 years or so—as cash gave way to checks, then credit cards, then ACH transfers, Venmo, PayPal, and Apple Pay—our "customer experience" *seems* to have gotten more streamlined. In actuality, though, as Twenty One Capital CEO Jack Mallers points out, it's only the front-facing user experience that's gotten slicker. The back-end infrastructure remains mind-bogglingly slow, complex, and (more to the point) *expensive*.

In other words, you might *think* you're cruising along a newly paved roadway, but you're *actually* slogging along a muddy trail.

⇢⇢

Let's consider a familiar scenario: you swipe your credit card at a coffee shop, grab your latte, and walk out the door. Simple, right? You paid $5 (thanks, inflation!) and went on with your day.

But behind that quick exchange lies a far more complex process. An intricate web of payment processors, banks, and settlement systems are working to reconcile your transaction. This global financial infrastructure makes it possible to swipe your card for a coffee in Rome just as easily as in your hometown.

But this convenience comes with hidden costs.

⇢⇢

While your payment feels instant—tap, swipe, done—the reality is far slower on the backend. Banks and payment processors often take days to fully settle these transactions, carefully reconciling balances and clearing payments. The seamless experience you enjoy at the counter masks a sluggish and deeply inefficient financial system beneath it all.

If it was just a matter of speed, that would be *their* problem. But of course, it's not.

Every step in this process comes with a price tag. You probably pay an annual credit card fee, monthly bank account fees, and— most significantly—the coffee shop pays a processing fee to Visa or Mastercard. These costs don't just disappear; they're typically passed on to customers in the form of higher prices.

It's a crowded transaction. Your bank, the coffee shop's bank, and multiple payment networks all take their share. Each layer adds friction, like mud slowing down a bicycle, requiring more money to keep the system moving.

In 2024 alone, merchant fees totalled nearly $187 billion—up nearly

9% from the previous year—costing the average American family almost $1,450.[97]

If you've ever donated to a nonprofit and had to decide whether or not to cover that 3% credit card fee, you've seen this charge firsthand: the more you donate, the more you pay.

There have been efforts to reduce these fees, but critics argue they're unlikely to meaningfully ease the burden on merchants—or consumers. Honestly, it's hard to expect otherwise.

But the stakes get even higher when we look beyond coffee shops and credit card fees. Every year, millions of people send money across borders to support their families—an act of love and sacrifice that often comes with a hefty price tag. The global remittance industry moves over $800 billion annually, but middlemen like banks and money transfer services can take anywhere from 5% to 10% in fees per transaction. For those sending smaller amounts, these fees can represent days or even weeks of hard-earned wages. So much devastating waste.

Bitcoin changes this dynamic entirely. Transactions settle quickly, securely, and at a fraction of the cost, ensuring that the sender's efforts aren't wasted and actually reach those who need the money the most.

With Bitcoin, whether you're sending money to family overseas, paying for a coffee, or buying a house, the network is blind to the value and purpose of your transaction. It simply transfers bitcoin directly from you to your intended recipient without middlemen or extra layers of cost and complexity.

↠

Before Bitcoin, we had no choice but to rely on financial middlemen, along with their fees, delays, and the inflated prices those costs create. Sending digital payments always involved third parties who took their cut, imposed restrictions, and left us vulnerable to fraud.

Additionally—though many are waking up to the enormity of the problem of constant corporate surveillance and monetization—as a society we've also become quite numb to their abuse of power. Our data is tracked, analyzed, and sold to unknown buyers so routinely that we've almost stopped questioning whether a better system is possible.

**This all stems from the way financial service companies make money**. First, they profit by lending us money, earning interest on credit cards, and sometimes charging annual fees just for the privilege of borrowing. Next, they profit during transactions, taking a cut through processing fees passed on to us by merchants. Finally, they profit after the transaction by selling our data, often without our knowledge or consent.

Bitcoin upends this dynamic. It's not a company. There's no CEO, no headquarters, no quarterly earnings calls, and no boardroom filled with executives brainstorming new ways to extract value from us.

**With Bitcoin, there's just you and me**.

⇥

You and me. It's almost strange to realize how simple this could be. You might make something—a handmade product, a piece of art, or even just offer a service—and I might want to buy it. In a world without these layers of unnecessary complexity, that transaction could happen directly, seamlessly, and without interference.

As political and economic anthropologist Natalie Smolenski said in her poignant keynote speech to a group of lawmakers at the 2024 Bitcoin Policy Summit:

Every great project—every great institution, every great discovery, every great company, every great country—begins with a *you* and a *me*.

There is no one 'we forgot to ask.' There is no one who can give us permission. There is no ID required. There is no third party. There's just you and me.

It's kind of amazing when such a simple concept has the capacity to blow our minds. "Peer to peer," Smolenski argues, is "a human right." And when you eliminate the noise, isn't that kind of freedom— the freedom to transact with one another—as fundamental as all the others?

-»»

We all still move through the world "peer-to-peer" in many meaningful and deeply human ways.

For example: when a friend has a baby, struggles with a health issue, or loses a loved one, we seek out ways to support them. We might organize a meal train, pick up groceries, or offer to babysit. These acts of kindness happen directly, person-to-person, without the need for an external middleman to manage, approve, or profit from our efforts.

These interactions are built on trust, connection, and shared humanity. Introducing a third-party intermediary into these moments would not only feel unnecessary, but would likely diminish their intimacy, making them feel cold, bureaucratic, and transactional.

At our core, we instinctively understand the power and beauty of peer-to-peer relationships; in a very real way—and strangely, due to its technical complexity—Bitcoin takes us back to that type of simplicity.

⇥

Bitcoin strips away the toll-takers, the gatekeepers, and the third-party overseers. It's just you and me, freed from the relentless siphoning of value that defines our current financial system.

If I want to send money to you—just like handing you a $20 bill—it shouldn't immediately be viewed as suspicious or nefarious. Yes, some people might misuse that ability for illicit purposes, just as plenty of financial crime takes place within traditional systems. (In fact, Bitcoin's public and transparent blockchain often makes illicit activity easier to track and uncover compared to the opaque nature of traditional banking networks!) But the potential for misuse doesn't invalidate the immense value of a secure system built on direct exchange.

The more suspicious we become of each other, the more society begins to unravel. Trust erodes, creativity is stifled, and our shared sense of connection weakens. Take a look around: is our current financial system fostering trust, innovation, and human flourishing? Or is it breeding cynicism, gatekeeping, and division?

⇥

For the first time in human history, anyone, anywhere—regardless of who they are or where they're from—can participate in a global financial network without needing permission from a bank, government, or intermediary.

This isn't just a *technical* breakthrough; it's a profoundly *human* one. It offers something our traditional financial systems have long failed to provide: equal access and true financial sovereignty.

That's why I'm so excited about Bitcoin. It's not just a tool for financial transactions—it's a gateway to a more open, inclusive, and fair global economy.

–»»

# Chapter 13 Summary

Like many early technologies, Bitcoin's early years have been marked by doubt and criticism. But it's not just a new payment system—it's a shift in how we move value through the world. By cutting out the middlemen who each take a cut along the way, Bitcoin brings us back to the original peer-to-peer nature of human exchange. We're no longer entirely dependent upon banks, payment processors, credit card networks, and other gatekeepers to give us permission to transact. This is particularly significant for the most vulnerable among us, largely excluded from that system, who bear its greatest burden. And as more and more people use the Bitcoin network, it grows even stronger, more secure, and more resilient—a virtuous cycle of strength and widespread accessibility.

**Key Takeaway**: Bitcoin enables direct, borderless value exchange without intermediaries, making it not only a store of value, but a network representing financial freedom. Bitcoin is the Internet of Money.

# 14.
# EVERYONE
# NEEDS
# HOPE

**"Injustice anywhere is a threat to justice everywhere.
We are caught in an inescapable network of
mutuality, tied in a single garment of destiny."**

MARTIN LUTHER KING JR.

---

THERE'S SOMETHING DEEPLY human about *hope*—it's what pushes us to endure hardship, build families, and dream of something better.

It's what drives parents to work long hours to give their children a better future. It's what keeps communities together in times of hardship and fuels the belief that tomorrow can be better than today. But hope can't be built on empty promises—it requires a foundation. And for billions of people around the world, that foundation has been systematically eroded by something most of us rarely stop to question: the integrity of our money.

⇥

In places where financial systems are crippled, money isn't just a tool; it's a lifeline. And when that lifeline is cut—through hyperinflation, government corruption, or arbitrary currency controls—it doesn't just affect bank accounts, it devastates lives.

Imagine waking up one day to find that the money you've worked your entire life to save is suddenly worthless. Imagine not being able to buy food for your family—not because you don't have money, but because your money is no longer accepted.

This isn't some distant, hypothetical scenario. It's a daily reality for people in countries like Venezuela, Lebanon, Zimbabwe, and Turkey—places where trust in the local currency has been completely shattered. Savings disappear overnight, wages become meaningless, and people are forced into impossible choices just to survive.

In these situations, the erosion of money isn't just an economic problem, it's a *human rights issue*.

⇥

But it's not just about extreme cases. Even in economically stable countries, cracks in the financial system are showing. When banks freeze accounts for political reasons, or when inflation quietly chips away at savings year after year, the consequences may be less dramatic, but they're no less real. Around the world, millions of people are waking up to the uncomfortable truth that the institutions they've been told to trust don't always have their best interests at heart.

This is where Bitcoin enters the conversation as *a tool for financial freedom*. At its core, Bitcoin isn't a speculative investment or a get-rich-quick scheme. It actually represents something deeply profound: a monetary system that no government can manipulate, no central bank can print into oblivion, and no authority can shut down. It's money for people who have been failed by their financial systems, excluded from economic opportunities, or silenced by oppressive regimes.

From activists in authoritarian countries using it to bypass censorship, to families in hyperinflationary economies preserving their savings in digital form, Bitcoin is quietly reshaping what's possible for millions of people. And in a world where trust is so often broken, it offers something rare and precious: hope.

→»

In the U.S., we certainly have our challenges, but our freedoms— our ability to pursue opportunities, express ourselves, and determine our own paths—have long served as a beacon for the world.

While we struggle with inflation and the sense of a fading American Dream, we rightfully celebrate our Constitutional protections securing "life, liberty, and the pursuit of happiness." The Constitution is a rare and wondrous achievement in human history, very much worth celebrating even as the work is never finished.

Widening the lens to our neighbors across the globe, we are quickly reminded of our own relative abundance: the fight for human rights is as alive today as ever.

→»

We talk a lot about basic rights and freedoms, but we often overlook one that helps safeguard them all: *the right to own and control our own money and property*. Without it, the others become far harder to protect. Without it, our ability to live freely is at risk.

When a government can freeze or seize someone's bank account at will, that person loses control over their own livelihood. They may be unable to pay bills, access medical care, or support their family. Their life rests in someone else's hands. As the *Journal of Democracy* put it, "In almost every dictatorship, the financial system is weaponized."[98]

For women living in over *one-third* of all countries worldwide,[99] such a lack of autonomy is a daily reality: they are forbidden from owning property, building businesses, or even leaving abusive situations. This doesn't just affect women economically, of course. Lacking economic freedom often corresponds to other forms of violence as well. In 63% of such cases worldwide, these women are mothers; the cycle of victimhood is almost impossible to break.[100]

In countries where governments dictate what farmers can or can't grow, they lose their autonomy and their connection to the land. The consequences can be devastating. In Bangladesh, for example, the government converted half of the world's largest mangrove forest into commercial shrimp farms to meet the conditions of international loans. This decision led to severe flooding, the destruction of fertile land, and widespread poverty and hunger.[101]

Under such conditions, people have no way of demanding any other essential rights and freedoms, either: dissenting journalists attempting to shine a light on corruption might have their offices raided or equipment seized. It's difficult to uphold freedom of speech without monetary freedom.

**In every society, property rights are critical to living freely and having the power to shape one's future**.

Or, as U.S. President John Adams put it, "Property must be secured, or liberty cannot exist."

The fact that many of us may not yet see the pressing need for Bitcoin might be a powerful indication of the freedoms and privileges we *do* enjoy.

⇥

I was raised with a real appreciation for those privileges.

My parents often described how, back in Poland, they did whatever they could to put away money. Saving from their wages was nearly impossible; whether you were a doctor or a teacher, everyone made a similar government salary, so people went to great lengths to procure gold jewelry, coins, and even U.S. dollars, which were widely considered to be the ultimate savings vehicle.

My mom would take my grandmother's earnings, trade her złotych (Polish money) for the currency of a nearby Eastern European country, and then travel into that neighboring country with hard-to-procure goods to sell on their markets. She'd be paid in local currency, and would then find travelers who'd change that money to złotych, which she'd then bring back into Poland.

The Polish had been navigating these waters for generations. When my grandparents were in their thirties—and dramatic inflation was an ever-present threat—the Służba Bezpieczeństwa (SB), a Polish government secret police force, would search homes suspected of holding U.S. dollars. One family friend, whose husband had escaped from Poland and sent money back to support their young baby, was betrayed by a neighbor: when the SB pounded on her door, she quickly shoved all of her cash into the baby's diaper and continued to bounce him, terrified, as the officers ransacked her apartment.

↠

I have thought about that mother so many times. When we hear that almost 54% of the world's population lives under authoritarian rule,[102] it's easy to miss the very human stories behind such abstractions. The sheer panic that mother must have felt—such experiences can never be communicated through statistics alone.

Behind the all-encompassing label of "human rights"—freedom of speech, freedom from slavery, the right to access basic necessities like food, water, shelter, and healthcare—are countless human stories. Real people are navigating day-to-day survival under circumstances many of us can hardly imagine, reminding us that these ideals aren't just abstract principles, but deeply personal struggles for dignity and opportunity.

⇶

Very few of us are entirely self-sufficient in this modern world; being cut off from money is the equivalent of being unable to obtain the basics that we all need to survive.[103] But most of us in the West take that financial freedom for granted. Even when we're stressed about our finances, we trust that we can access our bank accounts freely; exceptions are, at least for now, very rare and highly publicized.

We aren't worried that we might wake up and find that our money has become worthless—the "hidden theft" of inflation we've been exploring throughout the book is very real and very devastating, but it's usually more of a slow leak than a sword dangling over our heads, ready to fall at any moment.

When we want to start a business or organize our communities towards a political vision, we concern ourselves mainly with identifying the path to success and its potential obstacles, rather than the life-threatening dangers of trying.

In many parts of the world, such threats often strike together, as evidenced by the harrowing experience of entrepreneur Win Ko Ko Aung.

⇶

## Win Ko Ko Aung, Myanmar

Win Ko Ko Aung, a human rights activist born and raised in Myanmar (also known as Burma), grew up with no illusions about the fragility of his country's native currency. Five years before he was born, the Burmese military dictatorship demonetized its money, issuing a decree that approximately 80% of the banknotes would be removed from circulation.[104] Any money people had managed to save—tucked away in small safes, hidden under mattresses, or carefully stashed at home—became worthless overnight.

But it gets even worse, he says.

Everyone connected to people in power knew that this was going to happen. They started buying every hard asset they could—apartments, gold, land, you name it. Hard-working people had no idea that they were selling their belongings in exchange for a currency that was about to become little more than scrap paper. Most were financially decimated, and an entire generation was born into poverty. Win grew up knowing in his bones that fiat currency was pretty much "a scam."

⇶

By the time he was a young adult, Win managed to earn a substantial income writing a popular book. But always bearing in mind that the government could freeze his accounts at any time, he stashed his earnings in six different banks.

It didn't matter. By 2021, when he had amassed over half a million followers on Facebook, Burma seemed ready to fall to another successful military coup. Win encouraged his followers to join the peaceful demonstrations gathering in the streets, calling for a people's movement and demanding the release of political prisoners.

He soon became a "wanted man": his face was splashed across TV and state media, and all six bank accounts were frozen by the government.

But what the government didn't know was that Win's friend had encouraged him to buy some bitcoin, with advice that would soon change—and save—his life: "Do not trade."

Under the threat of imprisonment and torture, Win was able to disguise himself as a migrant worker and cash in some bitcoin to pay a human smuggler. He successfully escaped to Thailand with no documentation but his seed phrase (a security mechanism we'll learn about shortly) tucked away in his memory.

Once there, Win sold more of his bitcoin to sustain himself. He eventually made it to the U.S., where he now works with the Human Rights Foundation, helping to expand Bitcoin's capacity to support freedom and flourishing in places all over the world where people struggle against oppression.

When people start to understand Bitcoin, it's said that they've been "orange-pilled." Win didn't read a book or watch a podcast to become orange-pilled; as he put it, "It was the Burmese military that orange-pilled me."

This is why activists often say "Bitcoin is bad for dictators."

Oppression doesn't always come from corrupt leaders or internal conflicts within a country. Sometimes, it's built into the global economic system itself, which traps entire nations in cycles of debt and leaves ordinary people to suffer the most.

For many low-income countries, the dollar's role as the global reserve currency—established at Bretton Woods, as noted in Chapter Seven—creates a heavy reliance on U.S. dollars for international trade and loans. Even if these countries don't use dollars in their local economies, they still need them to buy essential goods like food, medicine, and fuel from other countries.

But there's a catch: these nations can't print U.S. dollars themselves. Instead, they often have to borrow dollars from international lenders.

To pay those loans back, they're forced to take desperate measures, like printing more of their own currency (which, of course, causes inflation), selling off valuable natural resources, or taking on even more debt. The cycle is incredibly hard to escape.

⇥

Let's take a look at currency debasement in this context—a pernicious and inescapable trap.

Imagine you're visiting a low-income country—let's call it "Country X"—with a handful of U.S. dollars. You'll probably notice right away how far your money goes. Meals, hotels, and souvenirs cost far less than back home. And if the local currency is suddenly devalued while you're there, your dollars will stretch even further. You might feel like royalty, at least temporarily.

The same holds true when we zoom out and think about economies as a whole. Let's say Country X took out a loan of $1 billion, which they are required to pay back in dollars.

No problem—through a simple accounting trick and the stroke of a pen, its government can simply debase the currency by half. Voilà! To accomplish this, the government prints more of its own currency. For example, if one U.S. dollar was previously worth ten units of local currency, printing more might push that exchange rate to 20 units per dollar. Now the government has effectively doubled its local currency supply.

This extra local currency can be used to pay government workers, fund projects, and cover domestic expenses, while the limited U.S. dollars are reserved specifically for repaying the debt.

But everything has its price. Printing money devalues the local currency, making it harder for ordinary citizens to buy goods and services since their money now buys, tragically, half as much as it did before the debasement.

In reality, the burden falls hardest on these people. Their savings are wiped out, their wages buy less food, and life becomes exponentially harder overnight. Worse still, governments under debt pressure often sell off land, resources, and labor at bargain prices to attract foreign capital and service their loans. These costs ultimately fall on the citizens.

**When people are stuck with a currency that holds no value outside their country's borders, its worth is entirely at the mercy of those in power, who can raise or lower its purchasing power as easily as turning a dial on a television.**

There's absolutely no recourse. All they can do is try and make do with half as much rice, coffee, and beans as they were able to purchase just yesterday.

--»

This reality has left billions of people trapped in cycles of poverty and dependent upon corrupt or restrictive governments with no other means to protect their livelihoods. In *Check Your Financial Privilege*, author Alex Gladstein of the Human Rights Foundation shares countless stories of this systemic injustice. He describes how nations will sacrifice their own people's well-being to pay back foreign creditors, often with devastating social and environmental costs.

In too many cases, a cycle of entrenched economic dependency is often greatly exacerbated by corrupt elites who directly benefit from these deals, while a powerless population is forced to face endless inflation, unemployment, and neglected, crumbling public services.

In Equatorial Guinea, for example, one-in-four children suffer from malnutrition, hospitals turn away those who can't pay upfront, and primary school enrollment ranks among the world's lowest.[105]

Meanwhile, the ruling elite has been documented diverting state funds for personal benefit, including purchasing luxury properties on multiple continents, sports cars (even a $8.4 million limited-edition Lamborghini Veneno roadster), jewelry, and Michael Jackson memorabilia.[106]

This story is all too common. And for centuries, people born into such a regime had no alternative but to try and survive within it; it takes resources to fight back, and soliciting such resources was nearly impossible under the watchful eyes of governments. To do so likely meant almost inevitable violence, imprisonment, and even death.

But not anymore, as visionary activists such as Farida Nabourema have discovered.

-»

## Farida Nabourema, Togo

In Togo, a small and scenic West African country, corruption runs deep. Government leaders enrich themselves at the expense of their people, and anyone who speaks out against the military regime can be imprisoned or tortured. Farida Nabourema, a prominent freedom fighter, knows this reality all too well. Her grandfather was beaten on the king's orders for distributing anti-government pamphlets, and his activism had lasting consequences. When the family was denied medical care in retaliation, two of his children— babies who would have become Farida's uncles—died in infancy.

Farida's father, continuing the fight, was in and out of prison throughout her childhood.

**At a young age, she learned the hard way that there's no better way to control a nation and its people than to control their money.**

As the oldest military regime in African history perpetrated endless crimes against the Togolese people—robbing them of their dignity, their livelihoods, and their dreams of self-sufficiency—Farida dedicated herself to learning about her country and its history of corruption.

She was determined to carry on her family's legacy, help topple the regime, and bring real self-governance to her people.

→»

Like Win, Farida's high-profile opposition eventually forced her into exile. But she persists, even knowing full well that she remains a target. As one Johns Hopkins University article puts it, "Farida Nabourema has been the face of opposition to the Togolese government—a dangerous role, considering the president's critics are often arrested, kidnapped, or killed."[107]

Farida often needed to send funds back home to support those fighting for democracy, but she had to find a way to do so that would go undetected. Togo's government has been tracking money flowing to activists and punishing people for "financing state terrorism."

That's how she discovered Bitcoin.

As Farida put it, "I felt a bit robbed of something when I started studying Bitcoin."[108] Like me, she hadn't learned soon enough how money works—not even at university.

Ever since, she's been a global voice in the push for monetary decolonization. People often ask Farida how a political activist fighting to bring down the oldest military dictatorship on the continent came to be a global voice for Bitcoin. Her response? Money *defines* politics!

Political victory, Farida realized, was not the only path to freeing Togo's people from the crushing weight of weaponized money. Political wins were essential, but could take decades to implement and entrench.

Farida's goal is now clear:

**"We want a currency that reminds us who we are," Farida says. "A currency for humanity."**[109]

⇶

I think of Farida often as I contemplate one of my own deepest personal missions: educating women about Bitcoin as a tool for true empowerment. Bitcoin provides a way for every woman—no matter where she lives and no matter how oppressive the government and culture—to achieve financial security and agency in her life.

And there's no better ambassador for the triumph of women under seemingly impossible conditions than Roya Mahboob.

⇶

## Roya Mahboob, Afghanistan

Roya Mahboob is not only the first female tech CEO in Afghanistan; she's also the entrepreneur bringing Afghani women into the world of coding and robotics, and bringing the world to them in return.

Her story is gaining widespread attention: she was named one of *Time* magazine's 100 most influential people,[110] and is now the subject of the 2025 film *Rule Breakers*, about her incredible journey from Taliban-controlled Afghanistan to the international stage with her award-winning Afghan Girls Robotics Team.

Roya doesn't just embody the unstoppable human spirit: she proves that hard work, determination, and hope are the true engines of change, even under the most oppressive conditions.

Her love affair with computers began when she first "heard about a shop that had small boxes that could communicate with each other."[111] Women weren't allowed in internet cafes, but Roya was so intrigued by the possibility of accessing a world of information that, with the help of a male cousin, she made it inside and got a taste of life beyond her own (very) limited experience. She was hooked.

Ever since, Roya's accomplishments have been dizzying: learning to code led to opportunities within her university and the Afghan government. Then she started a company—with her own savings—hiring 85% female employees, most of whom had never worked outside the home.

⇥⇥

Which brings us to Bitcoin.

Paying her employees was not as simple as it would seem. Cash was a problem because it might be confiscated by fathers, husbands, or brothers; ditto wiring money, since the women also couldn't have bank accounts without permission from the men in their lives.

In 2013, she learned about Bitcoin—it was priced under $100 at that point[112]—and it checked all of the boxes.[113] So Roya began to pay her employees in Bitcoin, many of whom were writing blogs and getting paid to tell their stories. For added comfort and confidence, she even assured the women that they could sell their bitcoin back to her at any time in exchange for cash (promising to buy it back even if the price plummeted, to make sure they'd never face a loss on their bitcoin). The payment system was successful: women became stewards of their own financial lives, which were, for the first time, entirely private.

Roya has since taught thousands of women about Bitcoin, believing it's the most world-changing invention since the internet.[114]

She said it perfectly: "Bitcoin gives them power. They can learn how to mine it, code it or trade it," she said. "When they earn money, they can convert that into radical self-reliance and power that they can use to escape the traditional role of Afghan women in the home."[115]

As Roya puts it, Bitcoin is "more than just an investment. It is a revolution."[116]

–»

*These stories are just the beginning*—thousands more remain untold.

For billions of people shut out of the financial system, Bitcoin is more than just a novel technology; it's an unprecedented opportunity to break free from cycles of debt and dependency that have haunted humanity for generations.

**In such places, Bitcoin becomes a sort of benevolent Trojan Horse. It quietly slips, undetected, under walls that had long kept freedom out.**

With just a phone and the internet, Bitcoin gives billions of people the chance to walk around the sealed door of economic opportunity.

Now *that's* hopeful.

–»

# Chapter 14 Summary

In many places around the world, people wake up to find their savings worthless or inaccessible. They have not only lost money—they've lost agency over their own lives. Bitcoin offers a lifeline. It has been used to escape dictatorships, fund resistance movements, and pay women who live under regimes that ban them from owning bank accounts. Bitcoin is a form of money that cannot be manipulated, seized, or printed into worthlessness, offering a pathway to dignity and self-determination for millions around the world.

**Key Takeaway**: Bitcoin is more than an asset. It represents irrevocable property rights and empowers individuals even in the most hostile regimes.

# 15.
# EVERYONE
# CAN BE THEIR
# OWN BANK

**"I hear and I forget. I see and I remember. I do and I understand."**

CONFUCIUS

ET'S BE HONEST: starting your Bitcoin journey can feel daunting. For many of us, it begins with a pain point—maybe it's the struggle of not being able to make ends meet, or frustration with a system that feels rigged and unfair. Could there really be a fix?

Someone suggests exploring Bitcoin, and we react with skepticism, maybe even outright dismissal. "It's too complicated," we think. "It's probably a scam." Life is busy, and the idea gets shelved.

But something keeps pulling it back into view—a news story, a price surge, or a comment from a friend. Even then, we hesitate, unsure where to start. And maybe we tell ourselves it's too late, kicking ourselves for not paying attention sooner. After all, the price has skyrocketed since we first heard about it.

Here's the truth: you're not too late. In fact, you're early. We're all early.

And let's clear up a common misconception: you don't need to buy a whole bitcoin. As previously mentioned, Bitcoin is divisible into 100 million parts, called satoshis, meaning you can start small, learn as you go, and proceed at your own pace.

This brings us to the heart of Bitcoin's potential: it enables you to be your own bank. In a world where trust in institutions is eroding and access to financial services isn't guaranteed for everyone, Bitcoin offers an unprecedented opportunity for financial independence and sovereignty. It puts control back in your hands, if you're willing to take it.

Let's explore how.

⇻

At the moment, there are four primary ways for people to gain exposure to Bitcoin:

1. **Self-custody**: Controlling your bitcoin directly by holding the private keys. You are your own bank, with full sovereignty over your funds.

2. **Custodial holding**: Entrusting a third-party exchange or service to hold and manage your bitcoin, just as you may hold most of your income at a commercial bank.

3. **ETFs and trusts**: Using traditional investment firms to invest in bitcoin indirectly through financial products, which can be held in accounts such as 401(k)s and IRAs.

4. **Equity**: Indirectly participating in Bitcoin's growth by purchasing shares in companies that hold bitcoin on their balance sheets.

Each of these paths offers a different way to get started, so explore your options and decide what feels right for you. Remember, this is just the beginning. You can always adjust and refine your approach as you learn more about Bitcoin.

⇉

Experienced, passionate Bitcoiners have strong convictions about *self-custody*. We have a mantra: "Not your keys, not your coins."

This definitely represents the approach that most fully embodies the spirit of Bitcoin we've been outlining in this book: when we self-custody, we're maximizing privacy, eliminating all counterparty risk (and all points of friction), and using and managing our money as we see fit.

As long as you have control over your *wallet* and *keys*—we'll get to those in a moment—you are invulnerable to the various problems that may arise when someone else is managing your bitcoin. These could include loss, theft, or an unexpected shift in regulations that changes the nature of your agreement with a third-party custody platform.

It's also important to remember that Bitcoin is a *bearer* asset. Like a dollar bill, it's owned by whoever happens to be holding it. A dollar bill doesn't have my name on it; if I drop it, it's equally useful to the lucky person who picks it up. Protecting your bitcoin is like protecting your cash.

As we've discussed throughout the book, Bitcoin was intentionally designed to be *decentralized*. Remember that inscription on the Genesis Block, about the chancellor on the brink of a second bailout for banks?

When money is centralized, control rests in the hands of the well-connected. They can grant and remove permission at will and print more whenever it's politically expedient to do so, regardless of the inflationary consequences. Decentralization is, therefore, at the heart of Bitcoin, and there's nothing more decentralized than millions (and, someday, billions) of people managing their money without interference or manipulation.

→»

Of course, with such freedom comes responsibility. Taking full self-custody of your bitcoin requires learning the ropes, and you must be extremely careful not to lose the keys to your wallet—because if you do, there's no institution to bail you out or restore access.

I know that can sound intimidating. But as you've learned throughout this book, the traditional banking system, while seemingly secure, carries its own set of hidden costs that often go unnoticed. You might find that the added responsibility of managing your own bitcoin is well worth the effort.

Think of self-custody as a journey rather than a leap. You don't need to dive headfirst; you can wade in slowly, step by step, building confidence and knowledge as you go. A gradual approach keeps the stakes manageable and makes the learning process feel rewarding and empowering.

Ready to take the plunge? Here are a few more things to know before getting started.

→»

Owning bitcoin means owning your place on the public ledger known as the blockchain. Bitcoin isn't a file or object that you can physically store or move between devices. Instead, it's a record of ownership tied to specific *addresses on the blockchain*—the decentralized, publicly accessible ledger that tracks all Bitcoin transactions. These addresses act like account numbers, showing where bitcoin is held and how much is associated with each address, but without revealing the identity of the person or entity controlling it.

A *wallet* is a tool that securely manages your *private key*, the cryptographic password that gives you control over specific addresses on the blockchain where your bitcoin is recorded. Think of the private key as your "digital signature" that allows you to unlock and send bitcoin stored at these addresses. Without your private key, no one—not even you—can access your bitcoin.

Remember in Chapter Eleven, when we imagined bitcoin being held in a "digital P.O. box"? This analogy is helpful in understanding how wallets work:

- The *public address* is like the P.O. box number—you can share it with anyone, and they can use it to send you bitcoin.

- The *private key* is like the physical key to the box itself, which you mustn't share with anyone and which gives you exclusive access to the bitcoin stored there.

It's important to understand that your bitcoin isn't "in" the wallet itself. The wallet is simply a tool for storing the private keys that connect you to the addresses on the blockchain that correspond with the bitcoin you own.

This might be one of the trickiest aspects of bitcoin custody to grasp. When people ask, "What exactly is a bitcoin?" or wonder if they can physically "hold one," the answer can feel a bit unsatisfying.

It's worth many thousands of dollars, but it's just an *address*?

Yes and no. Your bitcoin is associated with an address on the blockchain, but what it truly represents is *your share of the fixed 21 million bitcoin supply*. At any given moment, your private keys prove your exclusive control over that specific portion of the total supply that you own.

Think of it this way. Let's say, for instance, you owned a plot of land. Only you, and those you personally designate, are ever allowed to build on that land. In this case, your private key is like a deed designating your ownership, which represents your personal share of the total land in that region. Since nobody can physically create more land, your portion will always represent the same fraction of the total—a certain percentage of a permanently fixed supply.

→»

Naturally, you'll need to store those valuable keys somewhere. And as with physical wallets—you have options! There are many types of wallets to choose from, each offering different levels of security, convenience, and control. Some people prefer hardware wallets, also known as *cold storage*, which are physical devices designed for maximum security. Others opt for software wallets, also known as *hot wallets*, on their phones or computers, which balance convenience with security.

Hot wallets are called "hot" because they are always connected to the internet, making them convenient for quick access but more vulnerable to hacking. In contrast, cold storage wallets are kept offline, providing greater security by isolating your private keys from potential online threats.

Your choice will depend on your needs and comfort level as you begin your Bitcoin journey. There are also *multi-key custody solutions*, which are exactly what they sound like: they require several private keys to initiate a transaction, enhancing privacy and enabling members of a company or family to share custody.

→»

Hot wallets are good for beginners. They're easy to use, feel like any other app, and make buying, selling, and paying with bitcoin simple. They also work seamlessly with faster payment networks built on Bitcoin. However, it's best to store only a small amount of bitcoin in a hot wallet, as, again, they can be vulnerable to hacking or theft.

Cold storage is widely regarded as the highest standard for bitcoin custody. Since cold storage wallets keep your Bitcoin keys offline except when signing transactions, they are one of the most secure ways to store your Bitcoin.

Most people who custody their bitcoin in this fashion use a simple device, known as a hardware wallet, designed solely for storage of their private keys. The device often looks like a basic thumb drive, with a very limited interface (just a button or two) with which to enter the passcode and access the bitcoin.

It is recommended that people with cold wallets and seed phrases store them in an exceptionally secure place. Take it from James Howells, the man whose partner accidentally threw away a hard drive containing approximately 8,000 bitcoins (worth roughly $930 million as of this writing[117]): when it's lost, it's lost.

⇻

Whether you're using a hot or cold wallet, access to your bitcoin depends on your private keys, which are secured, as mentioned earlier, by a seed phrase. This seed phrase, typically a random set of 12 or 24 words generated when you set up your wallet, acts as a master key to your bitcoin. It's virtually impossible to guess, making it a critical layer of security.

Because the seed phrase is so important, it must be treated with extreme care. Write it down and store it securely—ideally in a different location from your hardware wallet if you're using one. For added protection, many people etch their seed phrases onto durable materials like metal plates to safeguard them against damage from fire or water.

No matter how you store your seed phrase, though, it is imperative to recognize that if it is lost or compromised in *any* way, you may lose control of your bitcoin. True sovereignty requires enormous maturity; an honest self-assessment of your capacity to manage this level of responsibility is crucial for successful self-custody.

The bottom line? Solutions range from easy but trust-dependent to highly secure but reliant on personal accountability.

**Either way, rest assured: with Bitcoin, there truly is an entry point for everyone.**

⟶

OK! So let's assume you've set up a wallet one way or another. Since there's no physical money changing hands, you might be wondering what's actually going on behind the scenes when you send or receive bitcoin.

Imagine you want to help a friend get started on their Bitcoin journey. First, you'd give them a copy of this book (wink, wink). Then, you'd help them set up a hot wallet on their smartphone, so you can send them $1 worth of satoshis.

Now it's time to initiate the transaction. Sending bitcoin tells the network, "Please move this much bitcoin from my address to my friend's address." The network verifies that you have enough bitcoin to cover the transaction and that you've provided your unique digital signature (the seed phrase that, again, only you know—your private key).

Since your bitcoin isn't a physical "thing," no objects change hands: once it's verified, the ledger—held on computers all over the world—will simply reflect that 5,000 satoshis left your address (your "P.O. box") and entered your friend's box, which was identified using their public key. The ownership has been updated.

That's it![118]

⟶

The fact that we've spent the bulk of this chapter discussing the intricacies of self-custody, reinforces—for all of the reasons enumerated above—the notion that this manner of holding bitcoin is most aligned with the Bitcoin ethos.

But there are certainly other ways to meaningfully participate in the Bitcoin ecosystem and reap its benefits, so let's briefly explore them.

Many people do not want to deal with protecting and managing their bitcoin. In this case, handing over the task to a *custodian* in the form of an exchange is a popular option. Companies offer services that make it exceptionally simple to get started: many are convenient, well-established, and regulated. Using an exchange feels no different, from a user experience, to using financial service applications like Venmo or PayPal.

High-profile cases of criminal behavior by some exchanges, however—most notoriously in the case of Sam Bankman-Fried and FTX—have highlighted the risks associated with storing your bitcoin with a third party, particularly those that operate offshore and don't comply with financial regulations. While many exchanges *do* operate securely and are fully compliant, keeping significant bitcoin holdings "online" is still not considered best practice due to risks like hacking and scams.

→»

Increasingly, large financial institutions are offering products that enable their clients to buy and hold bitcoin. The U.S. Securities and Exchange Commission (SEC) approval of "spot Bitcoin ETFs" in January 2024 unleashed a fresh wave of interest in Bitcoin among people who were interested in exposure to this high-performing asset but reluctant to initiate the process of procurement themselves.

Spot Bitcoin ETFs (exchange-traded funds) work just like regular ETFs, in that they represent investment funds that hold multiple assets in one place, but instead of owning stocks, the fund holds real bitcoin. Investors can buy shares of the fund through their regular brokerage account, making it easy to invest in bitcoin without dealing with wallets, passwords, or any technical setup.

This approval marked a significant milestone, as Bitcoin ETFs quickly attracted billions of dollars, outpacing even gold's early ETFs and solidifying Bitcoin's status as a mainstream financial asset.

This route has definitely proven appealing for more traditional investors, and the approval of the spot ETF has greatly expanded general awareness of Bitcoin. It is important to note, however, that such investments come with a price tag that self-sovereign bitcoin holders needn't pay: management fees and a potential haircut on the investment gains associated with straight-up bitcoin, not to mention the centralizing nature of such ubiquitous institutions, are worthy considerations in light of the decentralized ethos of Bitcoin.

⇶

At the moment, there are only a few public companies with significant levels of Bitcoin exposure on their balance sheets, although the number is growing every day. Under the visionary leadership of Michael Saylor, Strategy is a notable exception.

Entire books could (and will!) be written on the story of Saylor's groundbreaking strategy and the engineering mindset that enabled him to see, before virtually any other leader, the transformational power of Bitcoin.

Suffice it to say, for those individuals who would like to take a more well-worn path to profiting from Bitcoin, exposure through the purchase of shares in companies that hold Bitcoin as a treasury asset—and actively advocate for broader adoption—are also an option.

But don't forget: this is not the same thing as owning bitcoin yourself. The company's stock price is contingent upon many other factors, and may not accurately reflect Bitcoin's price action on any given day.

→»

As Bitcoin continues to grow, evolve, and mature, these avenues of adoption will adapt accordingly. Whether you want to take a "set it and forget it" approach or continue to study Bitcoin for years to come, the time you've spent orienting yourself in this ecosystem will be richly rewarded.

And not just financially: as we'll see in the last chapter—and as strange as it sounds—Bitcoin has a profound effect upon our very notions of time and purpose.

→»

# Chapter 15 Summary

There are many ways to start your Bitcoin journey. You can buy and hold it on an exchange, invest through ETFs, or take full control via self-custody. Self-custody most fully embodies Bitcoin's core principles of financial sovereignty. By managing your keys and becoming your own bank, you can avoid all middlemen and take direct control over your portion of the fixed supply. Bitcoin's divisibility into 100 million satoshis per coin makes it accessible to everyone, everywhere, regardless of budget or background.

**Key Takeaway**: Bitcoin can be owned by anyone, anywhere and anytime. From self-custody to institutional investment, there's a Bitcoin path for everyone. And each of them gives us unprecedented control over our own money.

# 16.
# EVERYONE WANTS A LIFE WELL-SPENT

**"Time is the most valuable thing a man can spend."**

DIOGENES LAËRTIUS

---

A S WE GROW older, we tend to re-evaluate our relationship with time.

What once felt infinite—lazy summers, endless weekends—starts to feel finite, even precious. In many ways, our time horizon shapes our decisions: whether we choose to save or spend, build or consume, invest in the future or chase instant gratification.

In our everyday lives, we often think of time in terms of calendars, appointments, and deadlines—the things we have to do today, and those that can be put off until tomorrow. We certainly zoom out a bit for bigger considerations—travel, event planning, our kids' educations—but for the most part, we slice and dice our time into manageable segments to stay organized and keep things moving. Time is a tool we use to coordinate our lives.

Stepping back even further, though, reveals the most basic truth about time: it's a measure of our limited number of days on Earth. Everything from our choice of careers to how we prioritize our family, friends, and leisure is ultimately a function of our relationship with the scarcity of time.

And few things affect our relationship with that scarcity more directly than our financial security and freedom.

-»>

Money certainly isn't everything, but it has a huge impact on the decisions we make. Anyone who has considered what they would do if they won the lottery—quit a job, buy a home, travel the world— can acknowledge money's immense power to shape our lives.

For me, fabulous wealth has never been the goal: like so many people in the U.S. and around the world, I have spent my entire life (except for one brief moment, in high school, when my parents bought that townhouse) living in small apartments. I'm not complaining: I am enormously grateful for all that my American upbringing has afforded me.

But for as long as I can remember, I've dreamed of owning a home of my own. Of not sharing my walls, floors, and ceilings with neighbors. A place of my own to maintain and create cherished family memories.

To me, that home represents hope.

-»>

Hope, when it comes down to it, is an expression of our feelings about the future: our own future, the future for our loved ones, the future of society and the world itself.

In other words, though we experience it *now*, hope is a future-oriented feeling.

For me, the possibility of owning my dream home provides great perspective on the present: if I *didn't* care about or believe in that future, I'd probably make different decisions. Why not splurge on an item of fleeting pleasure today, if saving for my bigger dreams was pointless?

Of course, it's not an exact science: to some degree, we are all subject to the demands of the present. This is a very intuitive process— we don't sit around measuring every choice we make in the moment against all future possibilities. But it's a real phenomenon, and economists have a name for it: the level at which we value present benefits compared to future benefits is known as our *time preference*.[119]

→»

Teenagers are often portrayed as having a very *high time preference*: one of their favorite expressions, YOLO ("you only live once"), points to things that might seem—to a mature adult—risky or irresponsible. A teen who discounts a sense of their future selves might be inclined to put their summer earnings towards a car, for example, over opening a college savings account, or to start smoking without any concern for their health down the road.

**High time preference is the prioritizing of current satisfactions over future ones.**

People with *low time preference*, on the other hand, recognize the value of planting seeds for their future selves to harvest. In earlier civilizations, this might have looked like the choice between fishing only to meet one's daily needs versus spending time investing in the construction of tools that will increase production down the road (such as fishing rods or boats). While such an effort might not pay off at first (they could be eating or sleeping instead of painstakingly building a boat), their future selves will be glad they did! In more modern terms, this might look like the difference, theoretically, between spending one's earnings on dining out instead of eating in and squirreling away the difference in order to save up for a home.

In both cases, the demands of the *current present* (literally right now) supersede the demands of the *future present* (the "now" that we'll only experience as "now," when we actually get there).

**Though it often goes unrecognized, the soundness of our money has an enormous impact on our time preference.**

↠

It's tricky: we tend to think that we only buy cheap things because we don't have enough money for the nice stuff, but if our money held its value—if you knew that your $5 was going to be worth at least $5 tomorrow, and maybe even $10 a bit further down the road—would you think twice about buying that $6 latte or cheap throw rug? Might you instead wait to buy the nicer one that would hold up over time, better reflects your taste, and was made with real care and craftsmanship rather than the one churned out in a distant factory?

If our money is strong—if it can hold or even increase its value over time—then we'll have a natural incentive to save, knowing that by sacrificing some temporary desires (an expensive dinner out tonight) we will make our future selves even happier (maybe an actual vacation someday?) and plan accordingly.

But the opposite is also true: when the money supply is being constantly inflated—causing our purchasing power to erode faster than we can make up the difference—we face a very real pressure to spend it now, before it buys even less for us later. The devastating effects of this condition are visible everywhere, from our own lives to global history.

*Hard money* resolves this tension in our system. It allows technological advances to naturally lower prices, without artificially offsetting them with the monetary expansion that perpetuates an inflationary economy.

→»

At its most extreme, inflation becomes *hyperinflation*. In countries experiencing hyperinflation, high time preference is a matter of survival: "Prices rise parabolically, which prompts consumers to panic-buy anything that will hold value and thus create massive shortages."[120]

In such cases, money becomes a hot potato, passed off in exchange for anything and everything as quickly as possible. In a hyperinflationary moment, as Saifedean Ammous points out, fruit trees are more useful as firewood now than for the fruit they will continue to bear year after year.[121]

Thankfully, most of us haven't experienced this tragic—and often deadly—economic condition.

But when we see hints of the same desperation in our own behavior, it's helpful to wonder whether the constant drumbeat of self-blame ("why can't I make better decisions?") isn't, instead, a function of the nuanced but very real effects of money that loses its value over time.

→»

The pull towards high time preference—spending now because money will be worth less later—isn't just about individual behavior, either. This tendency also has an enormous effect on how business is conducted, with implications that ripple far beyond the boardroom and into our daily lives.

Corporations are trapped in the same high time preference paradigm as the rest of us. They just operate at a whole different level, incentivized to maximize short-term profit and shareholder value over long-term sustainability.

↠

If you've noticed a huge shift in corporate culture over the last few decades, this helps to explain it. There was a time, not too long ago, when corporations had a lower time preference: they invested more in their employees, offering pensions and stable career paths that fostered loyalty and connection. They took great pride in building real things that would endure.

It seems almost old-fashioned at this point, but many in our parents' generation stayed with companies for decades—even across an entire career—knowing that their dedication would be rewarded financially (can you imagine having a defined benefit pension?), and personally. They cultivated lifelong relationships; they belonged to a work community.

Today, however, the opposite is true. The goal of short-term profits at all costs—driven by the need to keep delivering a return for shareholders within the context of rising inflation—has eroded that foundation. Transient and transactional relationships and disposable jobs (not to mention an entire gig economy of faceless, interchangeable workers) have been left in its place.

Examples of the destructiveness of low time preference abound. Fast fashion, fast food, and fast entertainment designed to appeal to the broadest possible audience—think of the movie studios that keep milking old franchises for a quick buck, rather than taking creative risks—give us a strong sense of what the world looks like when money can't hold its value.

↠

When we're stuck in a high time preference mindset, we tend to focus only on the short term. The future barely matters compared to what we need right now. For example, if a corporate executive is thinking short-term, dumping toxic waste into a river might seem like a quick fix. The product gets shipped today, employees get paid today, and the business survives another day.

But when that pressure eases—when our money holds its value and we don't feel like we're constantly racing against the clock—everything changes. Instead of seeing rivers, parks, and farmland as resources to grab before someone else does, we can start thinking long-term again. We can protect them not just for ourselves, but for future generations.

Lowering our time preference also changes how we treat each other. Instead of exploiting every opportunity for passing transactional gain, we build real relationships based on trust and mutual benefit. It's the difference between looting during a crisis and creating networks that last: when we value the future, we stop acting like takers and start acting like builders.

⇛

Which brings us back to the inevitable march of time in our own lives, and the way our financial landscape colors the choices we make.

Until Bitcoin, my dream of owning a home was almost impossible to imagine. I worked as hard as I could, year after year, but never seemed to come any closer to making it a reality. I put my personal life and the desire to create a family on the backburner. I tried desperately to save, and blamed myself for not being able to achieve my goals. I just didn't understand what I was doing wrong.

Now, of course, I understand completely: I was swimming against the tide. I was climbing a mountain that seemed to grow taller with every step.

Rather than wondering what I'm doing wrong, I now ask myself a completely different set of questions about the future: what would the world look like if everyone felt economically empowered?

What could people do with all the time they'd save if they didn't have to worry so much about affording their lives?

-»»

And what about you? If your money could retain—and even grow—in value over time, what would you do differently?

Do you love what you're doing for work, or would you make a different choice? Would you spend more time at home? Would you have more children? Travel? Would you learn the guitar, press wildflowers, volunteer at your local shelter? Would you read more books? Maybe write one?

What if we didn't have to work so hard to survive, and instead could work towards goals that gave us a real sense of satisfaction and pleasure?

Bitcoin has taught me to view money from a completely different perspective, and shown me that we can reclaim control over our time.

-»»

And speaking of time, it bears repeating: when it comes to studying Bitcoin, you're *early*. We all are.

As you can see in the global asset landscape depicted below, Bitcoin is still in its infancy. At the time of writing, it represents just less than $2 trillion of the $900 trillion total of global wealth. In contrast, real estate ($330 trillion), bonds ($300 trillion) and equities ($115 trillion) dominate as primary vehicles for wealth storage.

But predictions suggest that as adoption grows, significant capital will flow out of traditional asset classes and into Bitcoin.

**Figure 11: Global asset values**

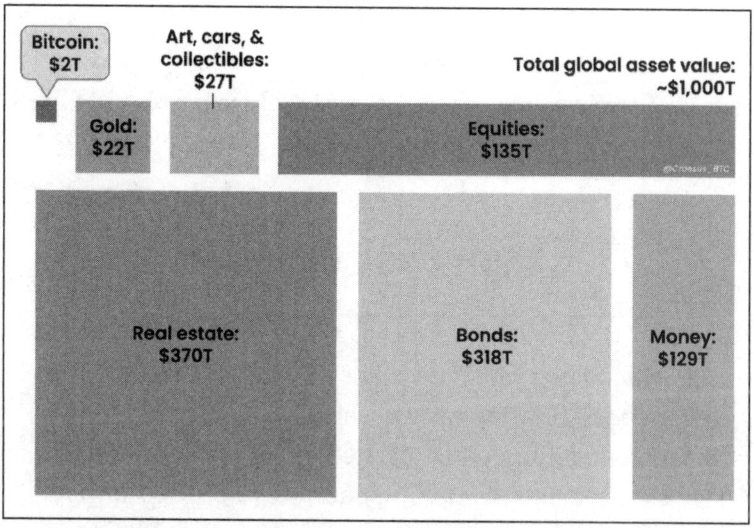

Source: Jesse Myers, "Once-in-a-Species," www.onceinaspecies.com.

Real estate could once again serve primarily to house real people rather than operating as a piggy bank. Art and collectibles might return to being appreciated for their cultural value rather than being prized primarily for their role as inflation hedges. With a monetary asset like Bitcoin anchoring global value, humanity can make the transformational shift towards a future-oriented mindset.

Imagine what such an awareness—not just as a moral imperative but as an economic reality—would mean to future generations.

When people are free from the anxiety of monetary debasement, they can invest their time, energy, and resources into building a world where long-term prosperity isn't just possible, it's inevitable.

↬

Bitcoin doesn't simply fix money; it fixes our relationship with time.

In this way, Bitcoin isn't just money at all. It's a reframing of the way money shapes our lives.

It's the best money ever invented to *store the energy of our work*. Instead of forcing us to chase it to survive, Bitcoin frees us to live.

→»

# Chapter 16 Summary

Our relationship with time shapes everything we do. *Time preference*—how much we value the future over the present—is an underappreciated influence on all of our decision-making. With fiat money, we're pushed toward short-term thinking: it makes sense to spend our money now, while it's worth more than it will be over time. This has enormous consequences both for our individual lives and for society as a whole. Bitcoin reverses the logic of short-term thinking: since it's scarce and deflationary, it encourages us to save and plan for the future.

**Key Takeaway**: Bitcoin realigns our relationship with time—it rewards patience and long-term planning by storing value across generations.

# EPILOGUE:
# BITCOIN IS FOR
# EVERYONE

> **"So the first answer to 'Why now?' is
> simply 'Because it's time'."**
>
> CLAY SHIRKY

ITCOIN IS AN idea whose time has come.

The digital asset may have started out with an obscure post on a message board for cryptographers, but it is now a household name across the globe. And while its complexity is indisputable— each one of these chapters could be its own book—its impact is a story that we're writing together.

I am passionate about Bitcoin not because I believe it has all the answers, but because it encourages us to grapple with some very important questions. How do we want to live?

How do we want to coexist with one another, and how might *sound digital money* help us achieve those ideals? Who are we, and who do we want to become? Why is it so hard to pause and ask these essential questions in our frenzied, distracted culture?

→»

The Statue of Liberty—and the American Dream she has come to represent—has long been a beacon for the world. Her torch has lit the way not only for Americans, but for people everywhere, like my parents, who saw in the United States living proof that given the right conditions, people could work hard, live free, and thrive.

It was not simply that America was prosperous, although that has certainly been key to its enduring legacy. It was also what that prosperity *enabled*: innovation and creativity. Community-building, civic engagement, and leisure time with family and friends. The ability to decide what we want to do, and the opportunity to go ahead and do it.

America today is *still* extraordinarily prosperous by any metric, but the upward mobility that was possible for other generations—at least with hard work and discipline—seems to have receded.

This is not because people have fundamentally changed; in many ways, it's because broken money has strained the American promise.

→»

Bitcoin revives not just the American Dream, but also our global economy and society at large. With Bitcoin, we're no longer breathlessly working to outpace an inflationary currency; with Bitcoin, we can slow down, imagine, and build a more humane and vital world.

By lifting a veil that had settled over Liberty's torch, Bitcoin casts the glow of opportunity far and wide. Light that had become concentrated on the few can now reach all of us, even in places where barriers were the norm and access strictly limited.

→»

It's ironic, in a way, that a new form of money emphasizing personal sovereignty can lead us into direct contact with a greater sense of society as a whole. No longer isolated within a murky, opaque system, we can see more clearly how deeply intertwined we truly are with people in our backyards and across the globe. We can see that a zero-sum game of winners and losers is not the only future reality, nor even the likeliest one.

Whether you're looking to diversify an already-robust portfolio or wondering how you're going to make next month's rent, Bitcoin is an investment in the vision of a future that we're not just *reacting* to but can actually *create together*.

Or, as Satoshi humbly and succinctly put it, "It might make sense just to get some in case it catches on."

Bitcoin is a rising tide, and it's poised to be the first money in history that truly has the capacity to lift all boats.

**Bitcoin is hope, and it really is for everyone.**

↠

# ACKNOWLEDGMENTS

Everyone has help along the way.

↬

Writing *Bitcoin is for Everyone* has been one of the most profound and transformative experiences of my life, and it would not have been possible without the support, love, and guidance of so many people who have walked alongside me.

First and foremost, I owe everything to my family. To my parents, who left behind everything they knew in pursuit of a better life for their children, I am forever indebted. Their courage to start anew in a foreign land, where everything was unfamiliar, shaped the person I am today. The sacrifices they made—never showing the weight of the struggles they faced—are etched deeply in my heart.

To my mother, who dreamed of a better world beyond the borders of Communist Poland and instilled in me the belief that anything is possible if we have the courage to fight for it. Her sacrifices fueled my desire to help others who are facing similar battles, and it's because of their unshakable faith in the American Dream that I strive to make that dream accessible to everyone. To my father, who worked tirelessly to build a better life for our family. I am deeply grateful for his quiet sacrifices and the love and encouragement he continues to show me every day.

To my dear brother, who faced so many challenges coming to this country at nearly 17 years old, and who has always supported me in following my dreams, even when they have taken me far from home. His warmth, optimism, and quick wit have long been a source of comfort and inspiration. I'm so very grateful to once again be near to him, his wife, and my darling niece.

To my late grandmother and grandfather, who taught my mother to dream of a life beyond the Iron Curtain, I owe much of the foundation of my perspective on freedom and opportunity. Their vision of a world where people could dream without limits has shaped not just my journey, but the stories I've told throughout my career.

To my husband, Sam Callahan, whose unwavering support and belief in me have carried me through the most challenging times, thank you. Your patience, understanding, and love have been my anchor. Your shared vision of a brighter future for everyone, one where financial freedom is a reality, has been a constant source of inspiration.

I also want to extend my heartfelt thanks to writer Allison Gustavson and my literary agent, Maura Phelan, who helped me transform my thoughts and ideas into the written word. Their dedication and expertise have been invaluable throughout this process. Allison, with her unmatched talent for the written word, worked tirelessly to ensure that my scriptwriting for TV found its voice in literary text. Together, they patiently sat with me, poring over every chapter, every word, and helping me refine my ideas in ways that I couldn't have done on my own. I am forever grateful for their guidance and skill.

I am profoundly grateful to my Bitcoin mentors. Their passion, knowledge, and commitment to creating a more inclusive financial world have deeply influenced my understanding of what is possible. Thank you for challenging my thinking and for helping me see Bitcoin not just as an investment, but as a revolutionary tool for empowerment. Notably, this includes Michael Saylor, Lyn Alden, Jeff Booth, Brian and Kelly Estes, Preston Pysh, Eric Weiss, Lawrence Lepard, Saifedean Ammous, Peter McCormack, and Lawrence Shea.

I must also thank my best friend of 19 years, Paula Pendley, whose steadfast support at my first Bitcoin conference helped me break into this new industry. Today, as a lawyer defending and championing justice for Bitcoin companies, she makes me prouder than ever.

To the many industry friends, colleagues, and brilliant minds who I've had the honor to connect with during my Bitcoin journey, thank you for sharing your time, collaborating side by side, and celebrating this extraordinary technology with me around the world. Thank you to Carla and Walker, Hunter, Nathanial, Teresa Bacal, Adam Back, Calli Bailey, David and Emily Bailey, Lynne Bairstow, Eric Balchunas, Haris Basit, Dom Bei, Sumit Behl, Aron Bender, Carly Benson, Marty Bent, Charlotte Bergmans, Nik Bhatia, Bill Miller, George Bodine, Joel Bomgar, Kelly Booth, Joe Burnett, Perianne Boring, Vijay Boyapati, Zach Bradford, Lee and Becca Bratcher, BTC Archive, Kaily Buemi, Bob Burnett, Joe Burnett, Joe Carlasare, Nic Carter, Vivian Cheng, John Christovich, Colin Coates, Renae Cormier, Alexandra Davani, Brian De Mint, Jason Don, Jack Dorsey, Julia Duzon, Sue Ennis, Charlene Fadirepo, Hong Fang, Efrat Fenigson, Fran Finney, David Foley, Silas Foley, Greg and Julie Foss, Martell Fox, Mike Germano, Alex Gladstein, Mike Germano, Simon Gerovich, Gui Gomes, Luke Gromen, Magdalena Gronowska, Dan Held, Stacy Herbert, Andrew Hohns, Matt Hougan, Hunter Horsley, Ella Hough, Lisa Hough, Adam Hurley, Neil Jacobs, Shirish Jajodia, Michael Jordan, Ed Juline, Andrew Kang, Max Keiser, Christian Keroles, Cory Klippsten, Tim Kotzman, Kyle Knobloch, Danny Knowles, Lyudmyla Kozlovska, Chris Kuiper, Victoria and James Lavish, Chris Lawlor, Shimon Lazarov, Phong Le, Dylan LeClair, Kiki LeClair, Nico Lechuga,

Tom Lee, Alex Leishman, Hailey Lennon, Parker Lewis, Stephan Livera, Caitlin Long, Jameson Lopp, Valerie B. Love, Jason Lowery, U.S. Senator Cynthia Lummis, Col. Douglas Macgregor, Roya Mahboob, Janet Maingi, Brooke Mallers, Jack Mallers, Sabrey Manning, Elina Marchenko, Matt Marlinski, Steve McClurg, Addie McDougal, Lana Miles, T.J. Miller, Brad Mills, Nico Moran, Brett and Sima Morrison, Mark Moss, Jesse Myers, Farida Nabourema, Nick Neumann, Eric Norris, NVK, Obi Nwosu, Matt O'Dell, Russell Okung, Thomas Pacchia, Jeff Park, Anil Patel, Raj Patel, Charles Payne, Matteo Pellegrini, Ben Perrin, Matthew Pines, Anthony and Polina Pompliano, Dennis Porter, Yan Pritzker, Demi Pysh, Brandon Quittem, David Rassiner, Will Reeves, Susie and TJ Reilly, Rick Rickertsen, Pete Rizzo, Bonnie Roberts, Samantha Robertson, Pierre and Morgen Rochard, Jeff Ross, Avik Roy, Becca Rubenfeld, Kimberly and Shaun Ryan, Isabella Santos, Anthony Scaramucci, Kyle and Anelia Schmitt, Trey and Cas Sellers, Eric Semler, James Seyffart, Lauren Sieckmann Wertheimer and Udi Wertheimer, Natalie Smolenski, Jimmy Song, Alex Stanczyk, Elizabeth Stark, Ross Stevens, Aubrey Strobel, Harry Sudock, Knut Svanholm, Aleks Svetski, Brady Swenson, Fred Thiel, Kristin Thompson, Alex Thorn, Vince Ungaro, Jeff Walton, Michelle Weekley, Ben Werkman, Jason Williams, C.J. Wilson, Tyler and Cameron Winklevoss, Cathie Wood, Tony Yazbeck, Eric Yakes, Endi Zekaj and Yujia Zhai.

My deepest thanks to my dear friend Ryan Tower for introducing me to Bitcoin in the first place, and to Larry, whose encouragement turned my curiosity into action—pushing me to read my first Bitcoin book and launch my podcast.

My heartfelt thanks go to my incredible friends, whose unwavering support has carried me through every chapter of my life. A special thank you Katie Banks, Samantha Cortese, Katie Corder, Kelli

DePaolis, Lisa Marie Grimes, Saphia Hall, Meghan Kluth, Lauren Sansone, Ariana Tejero, Jessica Tepas and Casi Ticer.

To the companies and teams whose partnerships have fueled my content and educational efforts, I am deeply grateful—your support makes my work possible.

To the immigrant community, whose resilience and hope continue to inspire me, this book is dedicated to you. I see in you the same drive, the same refusal to accept limitations that I have seen in my own family. Our stories are one of perseverance, of fighting to overcome systemic barriers, and of a belief that, with the right tools, we can create a future that is ours to shape.

To the pioneers of Bitcoin, whose work has inspired this journey, and to the people of all walks of life who continue to push for a more inclusive financial future, your work continues to drive my own. Thank you for your courage in challenging the system and for your vision of a world where financial sovereignty is available to everyone, not just the privileged few.

Thank you to Satoshi, whoever you may be. You have uplifted humanity through the gift that is Bitcoin.

And finally, to all of you reading these words, thank you. This book is for you. It is for the countless individuals who are tired of being left behind by a broken system and who are ready to embrace a new path forward. May you find hope, empowerment, and the strength to create a future where financial freedom is not a distant dream, but a reality for all.

This journey is not mine alone. It is one that is shared with many, and I am grateful for each and every person who has played a part in it.

↠

# GLOSSARY AND IMPORTANT TERMS

**ASICs (Application-Specific Integrated Circuits)**
Highly specialized computers designed to perform one simple function: mine bitcoin. ASICs solve the cryptographic puzzles that secure the Bitcoin network and validate transactions.

**Asset**
A resource with economic value—such as real estate, stocks, gold or Bitcoin—that can be owned or controlled with the expectation that it will hold, or even grow, that value.

**Asset Inflation**
A rise in the market prices of financial and real assets—such as housing, equities, or art—not due to increased utility or productivity, but as a result of excess capital flowing into these markets (in other words, "more money chasing the same goods"). This often occurs when newly created money seeks returns in investment markets rather than circulating through the broader economy.

**Bearer Asset**
A form of property—physical or digital—that gives whoever holds it full ownership and control. Cash is a physical bearer asset, and Bitcoin is a digital bearer asset.

## Bearer Instrument

A financial instrument that grants rights to the holder, without requiring proof of identity. Like a concert or lottery ticket, possession determines control.

## Bitcoin Public Address

The cryptographic identifier used to receive Bitcoin. Often compared to digital P.O. Box, a public address enables individuals to send funds to one another without revealing the recipient's identity. Public addresses are made up of a string of numbers and letters and can be shared freely.

## Bitcoin Wallet

A software or hardware tool that enables users to generate, store, and manage the private keys required to store, send, and receive bitcoin. The wallet does not hold bitcoin itself, but rather the credentials that unlock it on the blockchain.

## Blockchain

A distributed ledger that groups transactions into "blocks," each locked to the one before it by cryptographic hashes, creating an unbroken, append-only chain that's tamper-evident. Blockchains can be "permissionless" (like Bitcoin) or "permissioned" (managed privately).

## Block Reward/Block Subsidy

Newly issued bitcoin awarded to miners for expending real-world energy to solve the cryptographic puzzle and earn the right to validate a block of transactions and add them to the blockchain. The block subsidy is the primary mechanism through which new bitcoin enters circulation and serves as an economic incentive for securing the network.

## Bretton Woods Agreement

An international monetary arrangement established in 1944 that pegged global currencies to the U.S. dollar, which was, itself, backed by gold (until 1971). This deal institutionalized the dollar as the global reserve currency.

**Cantillon Effect**
A phenomenon, named for economist Richard Cantillon, that describes how newly created money disproportionately benefits those closest to the "money printer." These individuals and institutions have access to that new money before prices rise, while everyone else gets hit with inflation.

**Capital**
Capital is the buildings, machines, and tools that people invest in to produce goods and services, along with the money used to buy and run them. It represents savings set aside to grow businesses and earn future income.

**Capitalism**
Capitalism is the system where people use their savings to start businesses and compete freely in the market, driving innovation and economic growth. In this framework, profits reward ideas and efforts that create value, while losses help steer resources away from less successful ventures.

**Cold Storage**
Accessing your bitcoin through an offline "hard wallet"—via a USB-like device—is the strongest form of self-sovereignty available. Cold storage is considered the most secure way to safeguard bitcoin over the long term, akin to placing gold in a vault.

**Collateral**
Collateral is an asset you promise to a lender when you take out a loan—if you can't pay it back, the lender can seize and sell that asset to cover the debt. Common examples are a house for a mortgage or government bonds pledged by banks.

## Compound Annual Growth Rate (CAGR)
A measurement of the growth of an investment over time, providing a clear picture of long-term performance.

## Consensus-Based Mechanism
A method by which decentralized systems reach agreement on shared data—such as the validity of transactions—without relying on a central authority. Bitcoin uses proof-of-work as its consensus mechanism.

## Consumer Price Inflation (CPI)
An index calculated by the government to track changes in the cost of everyday goods—like food, gas, and rent. The CPI uses a standard "basket of goods" as a yardstick to measure purchasing power, but it is often criticized for understating real inflation.

## Cost of Living
The average amount of money required to meet basic needs, including housing, food, healthcare, and transportation.

## Counterparties
The parties on either side of a financial transaction. In traditional systems, intermediaries such as banks act as counterparties. Bitcoin eliminates the need for counterparties by enabling direct, trustless exchange.

## Counterparty Risk
The chance that the other party in a transaction won't fulfill their promise. Bitcoin eliminates this by settling value directly on its blockchain—once a transaction is confirmed, it's final and guaranteed by the network itself.

## Credit
Borrowed money that must be repaid over time, typically with interest.

## Cryptocurrency

A digital form of money that uses cryptography to secure transactions and regulate supply on a decentralized network. Bitcoin, the first cryptocurrency, remains the most decentralized and is the only one with a strictly limited supply.

## Cryptography

The practice of using math as a high-tech lock-and-key system to secure information. Cryptography uses math to protect digital information by turning it into a secret code, readable only by someone with the correct digital key.

## Curtailment

Losing excess energy—like wind or solar—because the supply is greater than the demand and existing infrastructure cannot absorb the surplus.

## Debt (Government Debt)

The running total the government owes to holders of its bonds. Each year the government may borrow to cover spending beyond its tax revenue—creating an annual deficit—and those yearly deficits accumulate into the overall debt.

## Decentralized

A system in which control and decision-making are distributed rather than concentrated in a central authority or single point of control.

## Deficit

A deficit is the shortfall between what the government earns (through taxes and other income) and what it spends. For instance, if the government collects $3 trillion in a year but spends $3.5 trillion, it runs a $500 billion deficit for that year.

## Deflation

A sustained decline in overall prices.

## Difficulty Adjustment

A built-in feature of the Bitcoin protocol that changes mining difficulty approximately every two weeks, in order to ensure that blocks are added at a consistent pace regardless of fluctuations in computing power or how many miners join or leave the network at any given moment.

## Divisibility

The capacity of money to be broken into smaller units for practical use. Bitcoin is highly divisible: each bitcoin can be split into 100 million smaller units called satoshis, allowing for precise transactions at any scale.

## Durability

One of the key properties of sound money: the ability to withstand physical or digital degradation over time. Bitcoin, like gold, is highly durable—it does not erode, corrode, or expire.

## Easy Money

Money that's cheap to borrow and readily available, often created in large quantities by central banks. Typically characterized by low interest rates and abundant credit, easy money can boost spending and asset prices, but also fuels bubbles and inequality.

## Equity

An ownership stake in an asset—like a house, stock, or business. Equity is what remains after subtracting any debt owed on the asset, and is a key metric of wealth.

## ETF (Exchange-Traded Fund)

An investment vehicle that tracks the price of an underlying asset and is traded on public exchanges like a stock. A Bitcoin ETF enables investment in Bitcoin through traditional brokerage accounts, without holding bitcoins directly.

## Federal Funds Rate
The benchmark interest rate at which commercial banks lend reserves to one another overnight. Set by the Federal Reserve, it serves as a foundational reference for interest rates throughout the economy, influencing everything from mortgages to credit card APRs.

## Federal Reserve (Fed)
The central banking system of the United States. It manages the nation's money supply, sets interest rates, and acts as lender of last resort during crises. While designed to maintain economic stability, its policies have come under increasing scrutiny for contributing to asset inflation and wealth inequality.

## Federal Reserve Act of 1913
The legislation that established the Federal Reserve System as the central bank of the United States. It granted the Fed authority to issue currency, regulate banks, and manage monetary policy with the stated aim of promoting financial stability.

## Fiat
Currency issued by a government that is not backed by a physical commodity such as gold or silver. Its value comes from legal status and public trust in the issuing government. Most modern national currencies operate as fiat money.

## Fiat Standard
A global monetary system in which fiat currencies dominate, created and managed by governments or central banks without commodity backing. This system enables expansive monetary policy, widespread credit issuance, and centralization of financial power. Bitcoin was developed as an alternative to this model.

## Financialization
The growing dominance of financial institutions, markets, and motives, overtaking real-world production. In a financialized

system, profits are increasingly derived from asset speculation rather than production of goods and services.

## Fractional Reserve Banking

A banking model in which institutions keep only a fraction of depositors' funds in reserve, lending out the rest to generate profit. This practice leaves banks vulnerable to "bank runs" when too many depositors demand withdrawals simultaneously, and is a significant contributor to the overall expansion of the money supply.

## Free Banking

A time period when private banks issued their own currencies backed by reserves, typically gold or silver. These decentralized systems operated without central banks and were subject to market-based checks and balances.

## Fungibility

The property of money that makes its individual units interchangeable with one another: a $20 bill is identical to every other $20 bill.

## Global Reserve Currency

A currency held in significant quantities by governments and institutions as part of international reserves and used in global trade. The U.S. dollar currently fulfills this role, granting the United States considerable economic and geopolitical influence.

## Gold Standard

A monetary system in which a country's currency is directly linked to a fixed quantity of gold.

## Halving

A pre-programmed event in the Bitcoin protocol that reduces the block reward for miners by 50%, occurring approximately every four years. Halving slows new supply and reinforces Bitcoin's scarcity.

**Hard Assets**
Investments with enduring value, such as real estate, precious metals, and productive land. These assets tend to retain value over time and serve as hedges against inflation and currency devaluation.

**Hard Money**
Currency that is difficult to produce or manipulate, typically due to natural or enforced scarcity.

**Hot Wallet**
A digital wallet connected to the internet. While ideal for accessibility and frequent transactions, hot wallets carry higher security risks and are generally recommended only for holding small amounts of bitcoin.

**Hyperinflation**
A scenario in which prices of goods and services rise at an uncontrollable pace of over 50% per month.[122] Hyperinflation erodes the value of money to the point of worthlessness, usually triggered by excessive money printing, loss of confidence in the currency, and political or economic instability.

**Interest Rate**
The cost of borrowing money or the reward for saving it. Central banks heavily influence interest rates, and those rates ripple through the economy, shaping how much people borrow, invest, and spend.

**Internet of Money**
A phrase used to describe Bitcoin's transformative role as a natively digital currency, allowing value to move across the internet without banks, borders, or centralized control. Just as the internet decentralized communication, Bitcoin aims to decentralize financial exchange.

## Ledger

A structured record of transactions. In the Bitcoin network, the ledger is public, distributed, and cryptographically secured. It is maintained by thousands of nodes to ensure transparency and prevent fraud.

## Lender of Last Resort

A function of central banks to provide emergency liquidity to financial institutions during periods of stress or crisis. While intended to prevent systemic collapse, this role can also introduce moral hazard by insulating risky actors from the consequences of failure.

## Medium of Exchange

One of the core functions of money: enabling the exchange of goods and services without bartering. For a medium of exchange to succeed, it must be widely accepted, easily transferable, and trusted.

## Mining

The competitive process by which Bitcoin transactions are verified and added to the blockchain. Miners expend computational power to solve cryptographic puzzles (see: Proof-of-Work) and are rewarded with newly issued Bitcoin (see: Block Reward) and transaction fees for securing the network.

## Monetary Inflation

An increase in the total supply of money within an economy. Monetary inflation dilutes the value of existing currency, often leading to asset bubbles and long-term price instability.

## Money Printer

A catch-all phrase referring to the ability of central banks to create new money, physically or digitally. While intended to stimulate the economy, this power can distort markets and erode purchasing power.

## Moral Hazard

When someone takes greater risks because they don't have to bear the full consequences. In finance, it often happens when bailouts, insurance, or other guarantees encourage reckless behavior by shifting the cost of failure onto others.

## Multi-Signature Custody (Multi-sig)

A security protocol that requires multiple cryptographic signatures to authorize a Bitcoin transaction. Often used by institutions or groups, multi-sig adds an additional layer of protection by distributing control among multiple parties or devices.

## Network Effect

A phenomenon in which the value of a product or system increases as more people use it.

## Node

An individual computer that runs Bitcoin software and helps enforce the network's rules. Nodes validate transactions, relay data, and maintain a full copy of the blockchain, contributing to the system's decentralization and integrity.

## Open-Source

A development model in which software code is freely available for anyone to inspect, modify, or improve.

## Peer-to-Peer

A way of exchanging value directly between people: no middlemen, no banks, no corporate infrastructure.

## Portability

The ease with which money can be transferred or transported.

## Private Keys

Cryptographic credentials—like secret codes—that grant access to a specific digital wallet. Whoever holds the private key controls the associated wallet; loss of the key results in permanent and irreversible loss of access.

## Promissory Note

A written agreement in which one party commits to pay another a specific amount at a future date. Promissory notes have historically served as the legal foundation for early forms of credit and currency.

## Proof-of-Work

The decentralized consensus mechanism Bitcoin uses to secure the network. Miners expend energy to solve cryptographic puzzles for the chance to validate transactions and add blocks to the blockchain (see: Mining). Winning miners receive newly issued Bitcoin (see: Block Reward) and transaction fees for securing the network through proof-of-work.

## Purchasing Power

The real-world value of money, defined by how many goods or services it can buy. As inflation rises or currency weakens, purchasing power declines.

## Quantitative Easing (QE)

A central bank policy involving the creation of new money—funneled through the banking system—to purchase financial assets, typically government bonds. QE is intended to stimulate lending and investment but often inflates asset prices and widens wealth inequality.

## Reserves

The portion of customer deposits that banks retain with the central bank. Reserves are intended to meet withdrawal demands and maintain liquidity, preventing bank runs.

## Salability

A measure of how easily and reliably an asset can be sold without losing value. High salability is a hallmark of sound money—it must be liquid, widely accepted, and resistant to volatility.

## Sats or Satoshi(s)

The smallest unit of Bitcoin, named after its creator. Satoshis are like pennies to a dollar. There are 100 million satoshis in one bitcoin, allowing for precise, micro-level transactions within the system.

## Scarcity

A condition in which supply—in this case, of money—is strictly limited. Bitcoin's maximum issuance of 21 million coins is enforced by code, creating predictable scarcity that underpins its role as a store of value.

## Self-Custody

The practice of maintaining full control over one's digital assets without relying on third-party custodians.

## Store of Value

A core monetary function that preserves purchasing power over time.

## Time Preference

An economic term describing how individuals prioritize present consumption over future savings. High time preference favors immediate gratification; low time preference favors long-term planning.

## "Too Big to Fail"

A term for institutions whose failure would pose systemic risk to the economy. Governments often intervene to prevent collapse, leading to bailouts, distorted incentives, and moral hazard.

## Total Money Supply

The total amount of money in circulation as measured in M2. This includes cash, deposits, and other liquid instruments. Rapid expansion of the money supply relative to economic output is a common driver of inflation.

## Triffin Dilemma

A structural problem faced by countries whose currencies serve as the global reserve asset. To meet global demand, the country must run persistent trade deficits, which ultimately undermines confidence in the currency's long-term stability. Since Bretton Woods, this dilemma has almost exclusively referred to the U.S.

## Unit of Account

A function of money that enables prices and debts to be measured and compared. For a unit of account to be effective, it must be stable, widely recognized, and consistent over time.

# ENDNOTES

1  John M. Griffina, Samuel Kruger, Gonzalo Maturana, "What Drove the 2003-2006 House Price Boom and Subsequent Collapse?" *Journal of Financial Economics* (September, 2021), www.sciencedirect.com.

2  Natalie Brunell, "Bitcoin ATMs in Sacramento! Wait, What's Bitcoin?" KCRA (November 19, 2017), www.kcra.com.

3  Inequality.org, "Wealth Inequality in the United States," www.inequality.org.

4  Madelin Brown *et al.*, "Nine Charts about Wealth and Inequality in America," www.apps.urban.org.

5  United States Census Bureau, "National Poverty in America Awareness Month" (January 2025), www.census.gov.

6  Inequality.org, "Wealth Inequality in the United States," www.inequality.org.

7  HBO, "Icahn: The Restless Billionaire" (2022), www.hbo.com.

8  Oyin Adedoyin, "Gen Z Sinks Deeper into Debt," *The Wall Street Journal* (May 7, 2024), www.wsj.com.

9  Mike Winters, "Over Half of Americans Have Medical Debt, Even Those with Health Insurance—Here's Why," CNBC (March 11, 2022).

10  Claire Thornton, "Food Banks are Struggling this Holiday Season as Inflation Creates 'Perfect Storm'," *USA Today News* (November 23, 2022), www.eu.usatoday.com.

11  NAHB, "Nearly Half of U.S. Households Can't afford a $250,000 Home" (May, 2024), www.nahb.org.

12  Tim Kephart, "25% of Millennials Currently Live with Parents, Survey Finds," *ABC Action News* (December 7, 2022), www.abcactionnews.com.

13  Dylan Sloan, "Larry Fink says Gen Z, Millennials Distrust Boomers on the Economy," *Fortune* (March 26, 2024), www.fortune.com.

14  Anthony Pompliano, "The Income Needed to Purchase a Typical U.S. Home has Increased by 79% in just 5 Years," *The Pomp Letter* (March 25, 2025), www.pomp.substack.com.

15 Aimee Picchi, "Retiring in America Increasingly Means Working into Old Age, New Book Finds," *CBS News* (April 18, 2024).

16 Michael Saylor, post in X, www.x.com.

17 Rufas Kamau, "Bitcoin's Philosophy and Political Promise of Borderlessness and Solving Inefficiencies," *Forbes* (October 6, 2022), www.forbes.com.

18 Bureau of Labor Statistics, "Consumer Prices Up 9.1% Over the Year Ended June 2022, Largest Increase in 40 Years," *The Economics Daily* (July 18, 2022), www.bls.gov.

19 National Center for Education Statistics, "Tuition Costs of Colleges and Universities," www.nces.ed.gov.

20 KFF, "2024 Employer health Benefits Survey" (October 9, 2024), www.kff.org.

21 Paul H. Keckley, "Analysis of Healthcare Spending Since 2000," Healthcare Executive, www.healthcareexecutive.org.

22 Federal Reserve Bank of St. Louis, "Median Sales Price of Houses Sold for the United States," www.fred.stlouisfed.org (accessed April 23, 2025).

23 Bureau of Labor Statistics, "Median Usual Weekly Earnings of Full-time Wage and Salary Workers by Sex," www.bls.gov.

24 Federal Reserve Bank of St. Louis, "Table data—M2" (Accessed April, 2025), www.fred.stlouisfed.org.

25 Mike Winters, Gabriel Cortés, "28-year-old made 15 offers, went $65,000 over asking price and still got rejected," CNBC (September 17, 2024), www.cnbc.com.

26 Julia Carpenter, "Why Young Adults Are Delaying Parenthood," *The Wall Street Journal* (January 7, 2022), www.wsj.com.

27 Sabrina Karl, "New Zillow Data Shows 'Typical Mortgage Payment' Has More Than Doubled in Just 5 Years," Investopedia (January 31, 2025), www.investopedia.com.

28 Board of Governors of the Federal Reserve System, "What is the Purpose of the Federal Reserve System," www.federalreserve.gov.

29 Christopher Leonard, *The Lords of Easy Money: How the Federal Reserve Broke the American Economy* (Simon & Schuster, 2022), p26.

30 Christopher Leonard, *The Lords of Easy Money: How the Federal Reserve Broke the American Economy* (Simon & Schuster, 2022), p26.

31 American Numismatic Association, "The History of Money," www.money.org.

32 Saifedean Ammous, *The Bitcoin Standard: The Decentralized Alternative to Central Banking* (Wiley, 2018), p13.

33 Saifedean Ammous, *The Bitcoin Standard: The Decentralized Alternative to Central Banking* (Wiley, 2018), p14.

34 Christopher Leonard, *Lords of Easy Money: How the Federal Reserve Broke the American Economy* (Simon & Schuster, 2022), p13.

35  Govmint, "Who Invented Ridges on Coins" (December 5, 2024), www.govmint.com.

36  Lyn Alden, *Broken Money: Why Our Financial System is Failing Us and How We Can Make it Better* (Timestamp Press, 2023), pp38-9.

37  Murray N. Rothbard, "Fractional Reserve Banking," *Mises Institute* (January 17, 2024), www.mises.org.

38  Lyn Alden, *Broken Money: Why Our Financial System is Failing Us and How We Can Make it Better* (Timestamp Press, 2023), pvii.

39  Lyn Alden, "Banks, QE, and Money-Printing," *Lyn Alden Investment Strategy* (November 2020), www.lynalden.com.

40  Christopher Leonard, *The Lords of Easy Money: How the Federal Reserve Broke the American Economy* (Simon & Schuster, 2022), p46.

41  Jon R. Moen and Ellis W. Tallman, "The Panic of 1907," *Federal Reserve History* (December 4, 2015), www.federalreservehistory.org.

42  Benjamin Wallace-Wells, "Loaded," *The New Yorker* (May 20, 2024).

43  David J. Erickson, "Before the Fed: The Historical Precedents of the Federal Reserve System," *Federal Reserve History* (December 4, 2015), www.federalreservehistory.org.

44  G. Edward Griffin, *The Creature from Jekyll Island: A Second Look at the Federal Reserve* (American Media, 1994), p5.

45  Phil Davies, "The Federal Reserve's Role During WWI," *Federal Reserve History* (November 22, 2013), www.federalreservehistory.org.

46  Hugh Rockoff, "Until It's Over, Over There: The U.S. Economy in World War I," National Bureau of Economic Research (June, 2004), www.nber.org.

47  Richard H. Timberlake, "Federal Reserve System," EconLib, www.econlib.org.

48  "Consumer Price Index, 1800–" Federal Reserve Bank of Minneapolis, www.minneapolisfed.org.

49  Christopher Leonard, *The Lords of Easy Money: How the Federal Reserve Broke the American Economy* (Simon & Schuster, 2022), p100.

50  "Trade and Gold Reserves after the Demise of the Classical Gold Standard," Federal Reserve Bank of St. Louis (September 1, 2020), www.stlouisfed.org.

51  "Bank Holiday of 1933," Federal Reserve History, www.federalreservehistory.org.

52  Franklin D. Roosevelt, "Executive Order 6102—Forbidding the Hoarding of Gold Coin, Gold Bullion and Gold Certificates," The American Presidency Project, www.presidency.ucsb.edu/node/208042.

53  "World War II," High Point Museum, www.highpointnc.gov.

54  World Bank Group, "Bretton Woods Monetary Conference, July 1-22, 1944," www.worldbank.org.

55   Lyn Alden, *Broken Money: Why Our Financial System is Failing Us and How We Can Make it Better* (Timestamp Press, 2023), p123.

56   "The Post World War II Boom: How America Got into Gear," History, www.history.com.

57   Levi Strauss & Co., "The Fall of the Wall: Jeans as a Symbol of Freedom in Eastern Europe" (November 6, 2014), www.levistrauss.com.

58   Tam Harbert, "Here's How Much the 2008 Bailouts Really Cost," MIT Management (February 21, 2019), www.mitsloan.mit.edu.

59   Josh Bivens, Elise Gould, and Jori Kandra, "CEO Pay Declined in 2023," Economic Policy Institute (September 19, 2024), www.epi.org.

60   Gaurang Dholakia, "Global Stock Buybacks Hit Record High In 2022; North America Drives Activity," S&P Global (May 25, 2023), www.spglobal.com.

61   Pallavi Rao, "Visualizing the $105 Trillion World Economy in One Chart," *Visual Capitalist* (August 9, 2023), www.visualcapitalist.com.

62   Jorgelina Do Rosario, "Global Debt Hits New Record High at $313 trillion," Reuters (February 21, 2024), www.reuters.com.

63   Fiscal Affairs Department, "Global Debt Monitor" (December 2024), www.imf.org.

64   Benn Steil and Elisabeth Harding, "For the First Time, the U.S. is Spending More on Debt Interest than Defense," Council on Foreign Relations (May 23, 2024), www.cfr.org.

65   Jeff Booth, *The Price of Tomorrow* (Stanley Press, 2020), pp2-3.

66   Aerospace, "A Brief History of GPS," www.aerospace.org.

67   Kate Ashford, "What is Deflation? Why is it Bad for the Economy?" *Forbes* (February 14, 2023), www.forbes.com.

68   Bitcoin, "Bitcoin is an Innovative Payment Network and a New Kind of Money," www.bitcoin.org.

69   Tim Ferriss, "The Tim Ferriss Show Transcripts: Nick Szabo (#244)," *Tim Ferriss* (June 1, 2018), www.tim.blog.

70   Rebekah Carter, "How Many Bitcoins Are There in 2024?" *Bankless Times* (May 6, 2025), www.banklesstimes.com.

71   Hass McCook, "Bitcoin's Energy Use Compared to Other Major Industries," *Bitcoin Magazine* (August 10, 2021), www.bitcoinmagazine.com.

72   Lyn Alden, "Bitcoin's Energy Usage Isn't a Problem. Here's Why," Lyn Alden Investment Strategy (August, 2021), www.lynalden.com.

73   Lyn Alden, "Bitcoin's Energy Usage Isn't a Problem. Here's Why," Lyn Alden Investment Strategy (August, 2021), www.lynalden.com.

74   Robert B. Jackson *et al.*, "Human Well-being and Per Capita Energy Use," *Ecosphere* (April 12, 2022), www.esajournals.onlinelibrary.wiley.com.

75  Gianna Lorenzato *et al.*, *Financing Solutions to Reduce Natural Gas Flaring and Methane Emissions*, (World Bank, 2022), www.openknowledge.worldbank.org.

76  James Larsen "Storage is the Key to the Renewable Energy Revolution," World Economic Forum (August 30, 2023), www.weforum.org.

77  Susie Violet Ward, "Bitcoin Mining Catalyzes Growth in Renewable Energy and Infrastructure," *Forbes* (October 18, 2023), www.forbes.com.

78  Stephen Alpher, "Marathon Teams Up with Abu Dhabi's Zero Two for Middle East's First Large-scale Immersion-cooled Bitcoin Mining," CoinDesk (May 9, 2023), www.coindesk.com.

79  Christian Sefrin, "Energy Transition and Bitcoin Mining: an Efficient Way to Stabilise the Grid?" Adesso (August 9, 2024), www.adesso.de.

80  Climate & Clean Air Coalition, "Methane," www.ccacoalition.org.

81  UN Environment Programme, "Methan Emissions are Driving Climate Change. Here's How to Reduce Them" (August 20, 2021), www.unep.org.

82  Robert B. Jackson *et al.*, "Human Well-being and per Capita Energy Use," *Ecosphere* (April 12, 2022), www.esajournals.onlinelibrary.wiley.com.

83  Mogomotsi Magome, "'What Can We Do?': Millions in African Countries Need Power," AP News (March 25, 2023), www.apnews.com.

84  Habitat for Humanity, "Energy Poverty: Effects on Development, Society, and Environment," www.habitat.org.

85  Alex Gladstein, "Stranded: How Bitcoin is Saving Wasted Energy and Expanding Financial Freedom in Africa," *Bitcoin Magazine* (January 24, 2024), www.bitcoinmagazine.com.

86  Liz Mills, "Bhutan's Bitcoin Mining Reveals Wider Interest in Digital Assets," Crypto Council for Innovation (October 2, 2024), www.cryptoforinnovation.org.

87  Daniel Ramirez-Escudero, "Bhutan's $750M Revenue from Bitcoin Mining Sets Model for Developing Nations," *CoinTelegraph* (September 20, 2024), www.cointelegraph.com.

88  Natalie Brunell, "The Untold Story of Bitcoin Data Centers Transforming Local Economies," YouTube (May 1, 2025), www.youtube.com.

89  World Economic Forum, "This Chocolate Factory is Powered by a Net-zero Bitcoin Mine," www.weforum.org.

90  World Bank Group, "The World Bank will Help Increase and Improve Access to Sustainable Electric Power in Rural Communities of Bolivia" (November 20, 2023), www.worldbank.org.

91  Alex Epstein, *Fossil Future: Why Global Human Flourishing Requires More Oil, Coal, and Natural Gas—Not Less* (Portfolio, 2022).

92  Rina Herzl, "Oxpeckers: The Rhino's Guard," Rhino Recovery Fund (December 29, 2021), www.rhinorecoveryfund.org.

93   Today, "'What is Internet?' Kate Couric, Bryant Gumbel are Puzzled," (June 20, 2019), www.today.com.

94   David Emery, "Did Paul Krugman Say the Internet's Effect on the World Economy Would Be 'No Greater Than the Fax Machine's'?" Snopes (June 7, 2018), www.snopes.com.

95   Zia Hayat, "Digital trust: How to Unleash the Trillion-dollar Opportunity for Our Global Economy," World Economic Forum (August 17, 2022), www.weforum.org.

96   Lyn Alden, "Analyzing Bitcoin's Network Effect," Lyn Alden Investment Strategy (March, 2021), www.lynalden.com.

97   J. Craig Shearman, "Credit and Debit Card 'Swipe' Fees Hit New Record of $187.2 Billion," Merchant Payments Coalition (March 18, 2025), www.merchantspaymentscoalition.com.

98   Alex Gladstein, "How to Dictator-Proof Your Money," *Journal of Democracy* (April, 2024), www.journalofdemocracy.org.

99   Roya Rahmani, "Ensuring Women have Equal Rights to Inheritance and Property is Key to Tackling Climate Change," Equality Now (June 23, 2022), www.equalitynow.org.

100   Alexandra Arévalo, "Economic Violence, a Silent Aggression," Friedrich Naumann Foundation (November 25, 2023), www.freiheit.org.

101   Alex Gladstein, "Structural Adjustment: How the IMF and World Bank Repress Poor Countries and Funnel their Resources to Rich Ones," *Bitcoin Magazine* (November 30, 2022), www.bitcoinmagazine.com.

102   Human Rights Foundation, "The Time for Democracy is Now" (September 15, 2022), www.hrf.org.

103   Michael Albertus, "How Authoritarians Turn Rural Areas into their Strongholds," *The Atlantic* (April 11, 2021), www.theatlantic.com.

104   The Irrawaddy, "The Day Three Myanmar Banknotes Suddenly Became Worthless" (September 5, 2019), www.irrawaddy.com.

105   "'Manna from Heaven?' How Health and Education Pay the Price for Self-Dealing in Equatorial Guinea," Human Rights Watch (June 15, 2017), www.hrw.org.

106   Katarina Hoije and Alonso Soto, "To Get IMF Bailout, Equatorial Guinea's Ruler Must Reveal Assets," Aljazeera (December 27, 2019), www.aljazeera.com.

107   Jacob deNobel, "Fighting for the Right to have Rights," Johns Hopkins University (November 21, 2019), www.hub.jhu.edu.

108   Block, Inc., "Currency of Freedom: Farida Nabourema and Jack Dorsey," YouTube (December 15, 2022), www.youtube.com.

109   Block, Inc., "Currency of Freedom: Farida Nabourema and Jack Dorsey," YouTube (December 15, 2022), www.youtube.com.

110   Sheryl Sandberg, "Roya Mahboob," *Time* (April 18, 2013), www.time.com.

111   Alex Gladstein, "Finding Financial Freedom in Afghanistan," *Bitcoin Magazine* (August 26, 2021), www.bitcoinmagazine.com.

112   Natalie Brunell, "Roya Mahboob: One of Afghanistan's First Female Tech CEOs on Bitcoin and Freedom in her Country," YouTube (October 19, 2021), www.youtube.com.

113   Alex Gladstein, "Finding Financial Freedom in Afghanistan," *Bitcoin Magazine* (August 26, 2021), www.bitcoinmagazine.com.

114   Alex Gladstein, "Finding Financial Freedom in Afghanistan," *Bitcoin Magazine* (August 26, 2021), www.bitcoinmagazine.com.

115   FIRST Staff, "Afghanistan's First Female Tech CEO on the Importance of Digital Literacy," FIRST (April 17, 2018), www.firstinspires.org.

116   Alex Gladstein, "Finding Financial Freedom in Afghanistan," *Bitcoin Magazine* (August 26, 2021), www.bitcoinmagazine.com.

117   Ryan Leston, "Man Says his Binned Bitcoin Fortune now Worth £500m," BBC (November 19, 2024), www.bbc.com.

118   For more information and up-to-date tutorials about how to begin your self-custody journey or purchase bitcoin on regulated, compliant exchanges, see my YouTube videos at www.shorturl.at/SRoWg.

119   Saifedean Ammous, *The Bitcoin Standard: The Decentralized Alternative to Central Banking* (Wiley, 2018), p74.

120   Jameson Lopp, "How to Prepare For Hyperinflation," *Forbes* (March 6, 2022), www.forbes.com.

121   Saifedean Ammous, *Principles of Economics* (The Saif House, 2023), p265.

122   Kimberly Amadeo, "Hyperinflation: Its Causes and Effects With Examples," The Balance (December 30, 2021), www.thebalancemoney.com.

# ABOUT THE AUTHOR

Natalie Brunell is the host of *Coin Stories*, the #1 Bitcoin podcast in the world. A leading voice in Bitcoin education and media, she's known for her powerful interviews, sharp storytelling, and ability to make complex financial topics relatable.

A first-generation immigrant and former investigative journalist, Natalie brings a unique passion for uncovering truth and empowering  people through knowledge. Her show features conversations with the most influential voices in Bitcoin and economics, consistently ranking among the top business-news podcasts in the U.S.

Natalie holds a Master of Science degree in Journalism from Northwestern University and has taught communication at the University of Southern California (USC). She also serves on the board of Semler Scientific, one of the largest public corporate Bitcoin treasury companies in the U.S.